# sweet &skinny

# sweet & skinny

100 Recipes for enjoying
**life's sweeter side**
without tipping the scales

Marisa Churchill

clarkson potter/publishers

new york

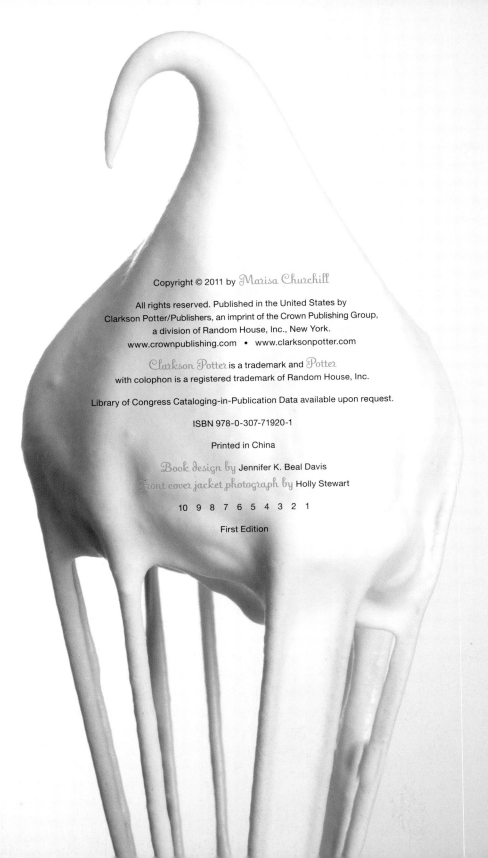

Book design by Jennifer K. Beal Davis
Front cover jacket photograph by Holly Stewart

10  9  8  7  6  5  4  3  2  1

First Edition

......................................................................

*This book is for my mother & father,*
who have been there for me every step of the way. I also
dedicate this book to my two amazing grandmothers,
and in loving memory to my *theia* Kiki. Μου λειπεις!

......................................................................

# contents

# Life is too short not to eat dessert.

In fact, dessert is often the very first part of the meal I eat. Rather than putting off the best part, why not start there?

After seeing me with a long spoon plunged deep into a dish of ice cream cloaked in chocolate sauce, people often ask, "How do you stay so skinny?" Well, enjoying life's sweeter side doesn't have to mean tipping the scales.

And looking good needn't mean a life of dry toast and cottage cheese. At five foot nine, I may have a little extra leeway, but, believe me, I eat plenty of dessert. After all, I'm inventing and preparing them constantly.

I am selective about the ingredients I use, eat sweets in moderation, and get plenty of exercise. In this book, I'll show you how to make dessert a guilt-free part of your life. As a professional pastry chef, I share some of my favorite recipes, giving you the skinny on how to start baking smart.

I will teach you how to substitute fat with ingredients that add texture and flavor so you won't feel deprived. Although these desserts contain less fat, they are still rich and satisfying. From simple techniques to clever kitchen tricks, *Sweet & Skinny* offers a path to eating healthier and baking simpler by lowering fat and cooking smart, with everything in moderation. In fact, you and your guests most likely won't notice that these desserts have less fat, fewer calories, and in some cases no sugar. You can enjoy everything from favorite childhood treats to contemporary dinner party desserts without guilt.

What could a pastry chef possibly know about healthy eating? Working in restaurant kitchens, I had to learn how to balance the fat, manage portion size, and maintain a healthy lifestyle. But my life lessons started even before I went to culinary school. Growing up, I was not a size two cheerleader. I loved to cook, and, even more, to eat! Eventually I learned to seek out ways to increase flavor and create healthier and lighter recipes, which led to a healthier and lighter me.

Later, working in popular San Francisco restaurants like The Slanted Door and Rubicon, I was making the typically rich desserts expected by restaurant patrons. By that time, I was slim and wanted to stay that way. How did I do it? By doing my B.E.S.T.—BALANCED diet, EXERCISE, SMALLER portions, and TIME to commit to these three things every day. For me, swimming competitively has been a big help. But with this book as your guide, you don't have to be an athlete to enjoy tempting desserts and still be your healthy B.E.S.T. It is this same philosophy that keeps me in tip-top shape for culinary competitions, like *Top Chef* and *Food Network Challenge*!

Baking the *Sweet & Skinny* way has opened doors for me, with *Food & Wine* magazine, Macy's, and others asking me to create reduced-fat recipes for culinary events. They wanted in on my secrets. Now, I share those secrets with you so that, with a little thought and commitment, but without deprivation, you can do this, too.

# keys to sweet & skinny desserts

Desserts rely on some specific scientific principles that help you to turn out moist and tender cakes, fudgy brownies, creamy custards, proudly puffed soufflés, and flaky pie crusts that crackle as you bite into them. I have developed tricks that bend the basic rules and ratios of baking and pastry-making so you can cut the fat and calories and still get it right. Here are my guiding principles:

Start with quality ingredients. As in all cooking, your desserts are only as strong as their foundation. For ingredients that contribute a lot of flavor, it's especially worth going out of your way, or sometimes spending a little more, for the best quality. Buy fruit from a farmers' market or a good produce store, for example. In The Sweet & Skinny Pantry (page 13), I share my favorite ingredients and tools for stocking your kitchen.

Look for good alternatives. In some cases, a lower-fat ingredient may be substituted for a higher-fat one without compromising flavor or texture. For example, while reduced-fat cream cheese has about 30 percent of the fat in full-fat cream cheese, and about 25 percent of the fat and calories in butter, it performs equally well when appropriately substituted in many recipes.

Learn the right technique. Technique contributes to both texture and flavor in desserts. In The Sweet & Skinny Pantry (page 13) and throughout the book, I share tips and techniques to ensure that your whipping, folding, and melting work perfectly. Mastering these basic skills will make cooking a joy.

Create contrast with texture. Contrast excites the palate. Think of a silky custard with a crunchy cookie topping, or hot chocolate topped with cool whipped cream. Some of my favorite tricks for adding texture are using crushed cookies and coarse sugars, and topping warm desserts with something cold.

Find the balance point. Balance is always important in cooking, but it is especially so when reducing sugar and fat. The primary balancing flavors in desserts are the same ones used in cooking: sweet, salty, acid (sour ingredients such as lemon and citrus), and bitter (think of coffee or dark chocolate). In this book, I explain flavor combinations and tell you how and why I've used certain ingredients to balance a dish.

Boost flavor with herbs and spices. Herbs and spices aren't just for the savory side of the kitchen. A bright bunch of fresh basil, a sweet spice blend, or a flavorful vanilla bean boosts the flavor and intensity of many of my favorite desserts.

Offer tempting presentations. First impressions are the most lasting ones. With the right presentation, your guests' mouths will be watering before they've even taken a bite. The photographs and simple tips here will help you to serve desserts that are as beautiful as they are delicious.

Reduce calories and fat. Calorie and fat information is included in each recipe to help you find desserts that meet your needs. This information is calculated using USDA standards and commonly available ingredient brands. Where there is a range of serving sizes, the larger number of servings is used to calculate the nutrition information. Where an ingredient indicates a quantity range, the smaller amount is used. Where two alternative ingredients are listed, the first is used. Where a brand name is suggested on the ingredient list, that's the one used in the calculation. Optional ingredients are not figured in.

Plan ahead. Look for Make Ahead! notes on many of the recipes to help you prepare all or part of the desserts in advance. Getting part of a recipe ready a day or two before helps make entertaining as easy as pie.

*Sweet & Skinny* provides you with everything you need to create desserts that will satisfy your cravings without threatening your waistline. So, what are you waiting for? Throw on an apron and start cooking *Sweet & Skinny*!

# the sweet & skinny pantry

Baking the *Sweet & Skinny* way requires some special attention to ingredients, techniques, and equipment. In this section, I share the essentials for stocking your pantry to ensure that your desserts taste fantastic, without a hint of compromise. At the end of the book, you'll find a resource list to help you find some of my favorite ingredients and equipment.

## IMPORTANT INGREDIENTS

With some products, texture, taste, and other qualities vary greatly from brand to brand. Throughout this book, I let you know when I have found that a particular brand makes a difference. These are my favorite ingredients for making desserts that work the first time and every time.

Sugar-free sweeteners. I have included a sugar-free alternative for selected recipes, using Truvía. Made from rebiana, the best-tasting part of the stevia plant, Truvía is the sugar-free sweetener that most closely replicates the taste and texture of granulated sugar, making it easy to use as a substitution. After working extensively with Truvía, I liked it well enough to become a spokesperson for the brand. It is widely available in supermarkets, packaged in boxes of individual packets and loose in jars. In most cases, you will be able to follow the recipe exactly as it is written, simply substituting the Truvía for the sugar. Where the method differs, alternative instructions are included.

Other sugar-free sweeteners may behave differently when mixing, heating, or baking, so you may need to experiment to get it right. A granulated rather than powdered or liquid product generally works best for baking.

Cream cheese. One of my favorite *Sweet & Skinny* tricks is replacing all or part of the butter in a recipe with reduced-fat cream cheese, also called neufchâtel. Dense cream cheeses work best to replicate butter's texture. The one I prefer, for both its flavor and its texture, is Kraft's Philadelphia brand reduced-fat cream cheese. Avoid brands that feel wet or gummy when you unwrap them; they often produce unsatisfactory results, particularly in pie crusts and shortcakes.

Greek-style yogurt. Yogurt is a great substitute for oil or butter in cakes. I prefer Greek-style yogurt for its thick texture and typically mild flavor. Thinner yogurts can affect the texture of desserts by adding too much liquid, and brands with a strong, tart flavor can overwhelm the dessert rather than contributing a pleasant subtle tang. There are many excellent brands of Greek-style yogurt on the market. My favorite is Fage (fah-yeh).

Chocolate. As a professional pastry chef, I have used Guittard chocolate for many years. Now widely available in supermarkets, Guittard semisweet chocolate chips have a rich chocolate flavor and are not as sweet as some others. But taste is personal, and if you prefer another brand, it should work equally well in these recipes.

Shortening. This solid form of vegetable oil has gotten a bad name because it is frequently hydrogenated, resulting in trans fats that have been linked to heart disease. Non-hydrogenated shortening, however, does not contain trans fats and so is a healthier choice. Shortening can help to create crumbly cookies and flaky pie crusts that may fool you into thinking they are loaded with butter. My preferred brand is the widely distributed Spectrum Organics Shortening, made from 100 percent organic expeller-pressed palm oil; it is not hydrogenated and is free of trans fats.

Oil. While the recipes calling for vegetable oil may be made successfully with canola oil or another mild-flavored vegetable oil, I tested them using Smart Balance Omega Cooking Oil. This blend of canola, soy, and olive oils provides 1,140 mg of omega-3 fatty acids per serving. It won't alter the recipe outcome if you choose another vegetable oil, but I have had good results with this one, and I like the added nutrition.

For recipes calling for olive oil, I prefer one that tastes of olives without being so strong that it overpowers the flavor of the dessert. I like Mezzetta extra virgin olive oil, but tastes vary and you should choose one with a flavor you like.

Butter. I prefer European-style butters, which contain less moisture than ordinary butter, thus improving the texture of desserts made with them. While these butters typically have a higher percentage of fat (82 percent or more compared to 80 percent in standard butters), for many of them, the difference is not great enough to affect the calories and fat per tablespoon. Because they deliver more buttery flavor, you can save on fat by using a little less. I prefer the flavor of Plugrá and Kerrygold brand butters, but I encourage you to taste the ones available in your area and choose one you like. Using Browned Butter (page 24) is one of my favorite tricks for enhancing butter's nutty flavor while using less of it, cutting back on fat.

Egg whites. You may notice that whipped egg whites are the key to reducing the fat in many of the cakes in this book. But did you know that egg whites create more volume when they are a couple of weeks old? The proteins in the eggs begin to relax over time. So save those fresh farmers' market eggs for omelets and use ones that have been in the fridge for a while for whipping up meringues.

Gelatin. Gelatin helps to create and hold texture in lower-fat desserts. It serves to stabilize and firm up many of the toppings, mousses, and puddings in this book, allowing you to use less fat but still have rich, creamy flavor and texture.

Spices. Cinnamon, nutmeg, ginger, star anise, and other spices allow you to make flavorful desserts with less fat. Sample spices to learn which varieties and growing regions suit your taste.

Vanilla beans. Whenever possible, I prefer to use vanilla beans rather than vanilla extract for their pure, intense vanilla flavor. This is especially important in reduced-fat desserts, where flavor is key. I have found that supermarket vanilla beans are often expensive and inconsistent in quality. I purchase my beans in quantity from Top Vanilla (see Sources & Resources on page 236). Because the beans can easily dry out, I pack about ten of them into a glass jar that's just large enough to hold them and fill it with vodka to cover the beans. Stored in a cool, dark cupboard, they will remain plump and moist for years. As a bonus, after about two months, the infused vodka can be used as a homemade vanilla extract.

Agave nectar. This sweetener, made from the agave plant (the same one that is used to make tequila), is a great way to add sweetness without using granulated or other sugars. Because it is a syrup, it dissolves easily without heating. Some studies have shown agave nectar to have a lower glycemic index than some other sugars; however, agave nectars each have their own composition, so if this is of concern to you, you might wish to do your own research.

## MUST-HAVE TOOLS

These favorite kitchen gadgets make baking a breeze!

Baking mats. I prefer reusable silicone baking mats to parchment paper, which must be discarded after one use. With baking mats, you needn't worry about cutting paper to size or greasing baking sheets. Baked items and candies won't stick, and the mats are easy to clean and easier on the environment. Silpat is the best-known brand.

Graters. I use Microplane brand graters for many tasks. The fine zester is perfect for removing the outer zest from citrus, and also works well for finely grating everything from beets to fresh ginger.

Kitchen torch. To caramelize the top of a dessert, I always reach for my torch rather than heating the broiler. It's more energy efficient, and it's a lot more fun. This is one case where you are allowed to play with fire! Look for small kitchen torches in cookware stores, or the less glamorous but more powerful (and often less expensive) propane torches in hardware stores.

Mixer. Because many of the recipes in this book rely on egg whites to do the heavy lifting in place of fat, they often require long mixing times, or mixing while slowly adding ingredients such as sugar and hot syrup. A standing mixer is the perfect tool for the job because you can leave it running, freeing up your hands to add ingredients or handle other tasks. Standing mixers typically come with both a paddle attachment, meant for creaming butter and similar actions, and a whisk attachment, for whipping air into egg whites, cream, and other ingredients. In most cases, a handheld electric mixer also works well, if a bit less conveniently. Some handheld mixers offer a choice of attachments; if yours doesn't, the standard beaters will do just fine.

Baking pans. I keep a variety of pans on hand in many sizes, with both regular and nonstick finishes. A springform pan is invaluable for easily releasing the cake from the pan, allowing you to unmold the cake without having to invert it twice to land it right-side-up. Muffin pans are perfect for cupcakes and other individual desserts.

Spatulas. Rubber and silicone spatulas are great for stirring sauces and folding ingredients into a batter. Heat-resistant spatulas are the most versatile, as they can be used in pans while cooking over high temperatures. For frosting cakes, spreading batter into pans, and similar tasks, you will want a metal spatula. I find offset spatulas, with their handles set off at an angle from the long blades, indispensable in the kitchen.

# TIPS & TRICKS

The following tips and tricks, learned over my many years as a chef, will help you not only in preparing the recipes in this book but also in your everyday cooking and baking.

Baking crusts blind. To bake a crust blind is to bake it on its own before it is filled, a technique often used for custard and other pies. Without the filling to hold it in place, the crust may slump into the pan or may puff up in spots while it is baking. To avoid both of these outcomes, fill the unbaked pie shell with pie weights or dried beans, such as pintos. Beans used as pie weights can be stored and reused. I store mine in a mason jar on the kitchen counter, and they have lasted just as long as my pie weights but cost me half as much.

Bringing eggs to room temperature. Many times, having eggs at room temperature helps them to whip to greater volume. To quickly warm refrigerated eggs, gently put them into a bowl and fill the bowl with hot tap water. Let them sit for just a minute and your eggs will be at room temperature.

Cutting cakes. To easily cut a cake into two layers, take a tip from Linda Carucci, Chef Director of the International Culinary School at the Art Institute of California–San Francisco: Put the completely cooled cake on a stand and wrap a long piece of dental floss around it, holding it against the cake in the center of the back side. Exchange the ends of the floss in your two hands so that they cross in front of you. Now, pull the two ends of the floss firmly away from each other to draw the floss through the cake, cutting it into two even layers.

soft peak

medium peak

firm peak

overbeaten

**Folding egg whites into dense batters.** When mixing together a light egg white meringue and a dense batter, folding can help you to combine the two without breaking down all of the air bubbles you worked so hard to create when you whipped the whites. Here's the technique I like best: Stir about 10 percent of the meringue into the denser mixture to lighten the dense mass. Using a rubber spatula, pile the remaining meringue on top of the dense batter. Plunge the spatula through the mixture to the bottom of the bowl, then scrape along the bottom, lifting and turning it up and over. Continue this folding motion until the mixture is combined. Occasionally as you fold, run the spatula lightly over the surface of the batter in a zigzag motion to reveal any hidden blocks of meringue that are not yet folded in. To avoid deflating the whites any more than needed, stop folding as soon as the mixture is no longer streaky.

**Making custards.** I avoid cooking custards on the stovetop unless I wish to infuse the liquid with aromatic ingredients, which is facilitated by warming. When working at Rubicon restaurant in San Francisco, I learned that custards cook perfectly well in the oven, and in fact have a silkier texture than those in which the milk and eggs have been precooked on the stovetop.

**Making meringue.** Whipping egg whites to the correct consistency is the key to recipes that include a meringue. By lifting the beaters, you can easily judge how much air has been incorporated into the meringue. Meringue beaten to a soft peak should be loose and barely able to hold a curl. For medium peaks, the soft curls of meringue should look like soft-serve ice cream. Meringue beaten to a firm peak should stand straight up in a point at the end of the beater. Take care not to mix beyond firm peaks, as the mixture will become dry, with the consistency of Styrofoam, making it difficult to fold into the batter.

Melting chocolate in a microwave oven. The trick to any chocolate-melting technique is to melt the chocolate until it is completely smooth without allowing it to scorch. Chop the chocolate into medium pieces and put it into a microwave-safe bowl. Heat for 20 to 30 seconds at a time, stirring each time, until the chocolate is smooth.

*Mise en place.* This French kitchen term means "everything in its place," and it is the holy grail of the restaurant industry. By setting up all of your measured and prepared ingredients before starting to mix them, you can work more efficiently and are less likely to miss a step or forget an ingredient. So, before you put on that apron, get out those mixing bowls and measuring cups, and prepare your *mise en place*!

Toasting nuts. Toast nuts on a rimmed baking sheet in a preheated 350°F oven for 7 to 10 minutes, until you begin to smell their aroma

Finally, always read through the complete recipe before you begin. And as you cook, look at both cooking times and alternative indicators. Oven temperatures and stovetop heat may vary, which means that cooking and baking times may be a few minutes shorter or longer than indicated in the recipe. Where there is a time range, begin checking at the earliest time and continue only until done as indicated in the recipe.

CHAPTER 1

# sweet foundations

With just a few baking and pastry building blocks, you have the foundation for a variety of *Sweet & Skinny* desserts. From flaky pie crust, to tender sugar-free cakes, to creamy sauces and fluffy toppings, these essential elements are used throughout this book. But please don't stop with the recipes included here. These sweet foundations can help you to expand your repertoire by substituting *Sweet & Skinny* crusts, toppings, and sauces in all of your favorite recipes. This chapter gives you the tools to create your own sweet treats the *Sweet & Skinny* way.

# Browned Butter

1 cup (2 sticks) unsalted butter, cut into ½-inch-thick slices

Also known by its French name, *beurre noisette,* browned butter is made by heating butter until all of its moisture evaporates and the milk solids begin to brown. It's a great trick to have up your sleeve for low-fat baking because it boosts the butter's flavor, making it nutty and complex. This allows you to use less fat and still have plenty of rich, buttery flavor. I make browned butter a cup or more at a time so I always have some on hand.

"Softened" browned butter, called for in some recipes, will have a slightly softer consistency than softened butter.

MAKE AHEAD!

The browned butter can be refrigerated in an airtight container for several weeks, or frozen for up to 2 months. Thaw frozen butter overnight in the refrigerator.

In a medium saucepan, heat the butter over medium heat, stirring occasionally, until it melts and begins to foam. Once it begins to brown, stir continuously with a heatproof spatula to prevent the milk solids from burning. Continue to cook until the butter turns golden and you detect a nutty aroma.

Scrape the butter into a small bowl, cover, and refrigerate for several hours, until it is firm.

To quickly chill the browned butter for a recipe, pour the amount you will need into a baking pan or saucepan so that it is in a thin layer. Freeze for about 15 minutes, until the butter is firm.

# Quick Graham Cracker Crust

Nonstick pan spray

6 ounces honey graham crackers (about 10 cookie sheets)

2 tablespoons 1% or 2% milk

This may be the quickest way possible to make a crust—even faster than running out to the store for a ready-made one! No one will ever know you snuck in milk in place of the butter. The crust does well without baking before filling. For a recipe requiring a prebaked crust, follow the recipe instructions for baking.

Coat a 9-inch springform pan or round cake pan with pan spray. Break up the graham crackers and process them in a food processor until they are reduced to very fine crumbs. Add the milk and process for 30 seconds, or until the crumbs hold together when you squeeze them in your fist.

Transfer the mixture to the prepared pan. Press the crumbs firmly over the bottom and slightly up the sides of the pan, using your fingertips or the bottom of a glass to help compress them.

Fill and bake according to the recipe.

# Cream Cheese Pie Crust

Nonstick pan spray

3 ounces (6 tablespoons) Kraft reduced-fat cream cheese (neufchâtel), cold, cut into ¼-inch cubes

3 tablespoons unsalted butter, cold, cut into ¼-inch cubes

3½ tablespoons water, ice-cold

1½ teaspoons white vinegar or fresh lemon juice, ice-cold

1 cup plus 2 tablespoons cake flour

1 teaspoon sugar (optional)

¼ teaspoon baking powder

⅛ teaspoon salt

MAKE AHEAD!

The crust can be refrigerated in the pan, covered with plastic film, for up to 2 days before baking.

Pie crust can be tricky when baking skinny because it is the fat that gives a crust its flaky texture. By freezing the butter and cream cheese until they are very cold and firm, I have gotten them to work overtime, contributing every bit of flakiness they've got. While you generally want to avoid overmixing pastry dough, in this case you mix it a bit longer for the best texture. The small amount of sugar may be omitted for a sugar-free crust.

Preheat the oven to 375°F with a rack in the center position. Generously coat a 9-inch pie pan with pan spray.

Arrange the cream cheese and butter in a single layer on separate plates or pieces of waxed paper. Freeze for 30 to 40 minutes, until they are firm.

Remove the frozen cream cheese from the freezer (leave the butter); set aside. In a small bowl, stir together the water and vinegar; refrigerate.

Using a standing mixer fitted with the paddle attachment, mix the flour, sugar (if using), baking powder, and salt on low speed to combine them. Add the cream cheese and mix on medium-low for 2 minutes. Add the frozen butter and continue mixing until the cream cheese and butter are in pebble-size pieces. (Alternatively, use a bowl and a pastry cutter or two knives.)

With the mixer on low, add the vinegar mixture and blend until the dough begins to ball up around the paddle. (If mixing by hand, toss in the liquid with a fork.) Continue to mix for 1 minute after the dough has formed.

Transfer the dough to a lightly floured surface and roll it between two sheets of plastic film to form a 13-inch round about $1/8$ inch thick. (Roll to a $1/16$-inch thickness if making a lattice top.) Remove the top film and invert the dough over a 9-inch pie or tart pan, or as indicated in the recipe you are using. Remove the film and press the dough firmly onto the bottom and sides of the pan. Trim away the excess dough. (If making a lattice top, save the scraps.)

Refrigerate the crust, covered with plastic film, for at least 30 minutes.

If making a lattice top, reroll the scraps into a $1/16$-inch-thick disk. Cut it into ten $1/2$-inch-wide strips, using a pastry wheel, pizza cutter, or sharp knife. Place the strips on a baking sheet that has been coated with pan spray. Cover the strips lightly with plastic film, and refrigerate.

To bake the crust blind (unfilled), cut a piece of aluminum foil that is large enough to cover the crust and coat it with pan spray. Put it coated-side-down on the crust and press to mold it to the shape of the pan. Pour in beans or pie weights to fill the pan (this will prevent the crust from shrinking as it bakes). Bake for 30 minutes, or until the crust is cooked through but has not yet begun to brown. Set aside to cool.

To finish a filled crust with a lattice top, evenly space 5 strips over the filling, running vertically, and press the ends of each strip firmly against the bottom crust to seal them. Lay 5 strips across the first at an angle, again spacing them evenly. Press to seal. Bake the filled tart or pie according to the recipe instructions.

# Shortbread Cookie Crust

MAKES ONE 9- OR 10-INCH CRUST

PER SERVING (12 TO 16 SERVINGS): 60 CALORIES, 3.5 GRAMS FAT
PER SERVING (SUGAR FREE): 45 CALORIES, 3.5 GRAMS FAT

Nonstick pan spray

¼ cup Browned Butter (page 24), softened

1 tablespoon reduced-fat cream cheese (neufchâtel)

2 teaspoons non-hydrogenated shortening, such as Spectrum brand

2 tablespoons powdered sugar

1 tablespoon liquid egg substitute

1 teaspoon pure vanilla extract

1 cup all-purpose flour

⅛ teaspoon salt

**MAKE AHEAD!**

The crumbs can be stored in a resealable plastic bag at room temperature for up to 1 week, or frozen for up to 3 weeks. Thaw frozen crumbs overnight at room temperature before using.

**SWEET & SUGAR FREE!**

Substitute 1 tablespoon plus 2 teaspoons (6 packets) of Truvía for the powdered sugar.

This buttery crust is based on my *yiayia*'s (grandmother's) Kourabiethes (page 121)—my favorite Greek butter cookie. It is the perfect crust for cheesecakes, bar cookies, and many other desserts. Because of the sugar-free option, it's a great choice for a sugar-free cheesecake.

Preheat the oven to 350°F with a rack in the center position. Coat a baking sheet with pan spray.

Using a standing mixer fitted with the paddle attachment, beat the butter, cream cheese, shortening, and powdered sugar together on medium speed for 10 minutes. (Alternatively, use a handheld electric mixer.) Add the egg substitute and vanilla; beat for 2 minutes longer. Add the flour and salt; mix for 10 minutes more.

Transfer the dough to a lightly floured surface and pat it into a ½-inch-thick disk. Cut the dough into 4 strips in one direction, then 4 in the other, to make 16 pieces.

Transfer the cookies to the prepared baking sheet, placing them ½ inch apart (they will not spread). Bake for 30 minutes, or until the bottoms are golden. Transfer the cookies directly to a wire rack and let them cool completely, about 1 hour.

Process the cooled cookies in a food processor until they have the consistency of sand.

Press the crumbs into the bottom of the pan specified in the recipe. Fill and bake according to the recipe.

# Graham Cracker Pie Crust

Nonstick pan spray

6 ounces honey graham crackers (about 10 cookie sheets)

3 tablespoons (packed) dark brown sugar

2 tablespoons all-purpose flour

½ teaspoon salt

¼ cup (½ stick) unsalted butter

2 teaspoons non-hydrogenated shortening, such as Spectrum brand

This crust works well for custard-based pies. It's easy to make and tastes wonderfully rich. Graham crackers are naturally low in fat, so I prefer to use the full-fat ones rather than the reduced-fat graham crackers, which have an artificial taste.

Generously coat a pie or tart pan with pan spray.

Crumble the graham crackers into a food processor and process until they are reduced to very fine crumbs. Add the brown sugar, flour, and salt and process for 30 seconds.

In a small saucepan, or in the microwave, melt the butter and shortening. Pour it over the graham cracker mixture, start the food processor running, and drizzle in 3 tablespoons water through the feed tube, mixing until the mixture clumps up around the blade. The dough should easily hold together when you pinch off a clump. If it does not, add 2 to 3 teaspoons more water, pulse to combine, and try pinching it again.

Roll the dough between sheets of plastic film to form a round that is ⅛ inch thick and approximately 13 inches in diameter. Remove the top film and invert the dough, centering it over the prepared pan. Gently press the dough into the pan, using the top film as an aid. Peel off the film and continue to press the crust to cover the bottom and sides of the pan. Trim away any excess dough from the edges. If the crust cracks or tears, use scraps of dough to repair it, pressing to seal the cracks.

recipe continues

The unbaked crust can be frozen, wrapped tightly in plastic film, for up to 2 weeks in advance. Transfer it to the refrigerator the night before baking. The baked crust can be stored at room temperature, covered with plastic film, for up to 24 hours before filling.

Freeze the crust for 20 minutes, or until it is firm to the touch but not frozen through.

Meanwhile, preheat the oven to 350°F with a rack in the center position.

Prick the bottom of the crust all over with a fork. Bake for 25 to 30 minutes, until the edges are golden brown and the bottom is cooked through and no longer appears shiny.

Let the crust cool in the pan for at least 2 hours.

To Form Individual Tarts   Use a round cutter or a sharp knife to cut the dough into six 4½-inch rounds. (You will need to gather and reroll the scraps to make the final 2 rounds.) Peel the rounds from the film and press them evenly into the pans. The baking time will be about the same.

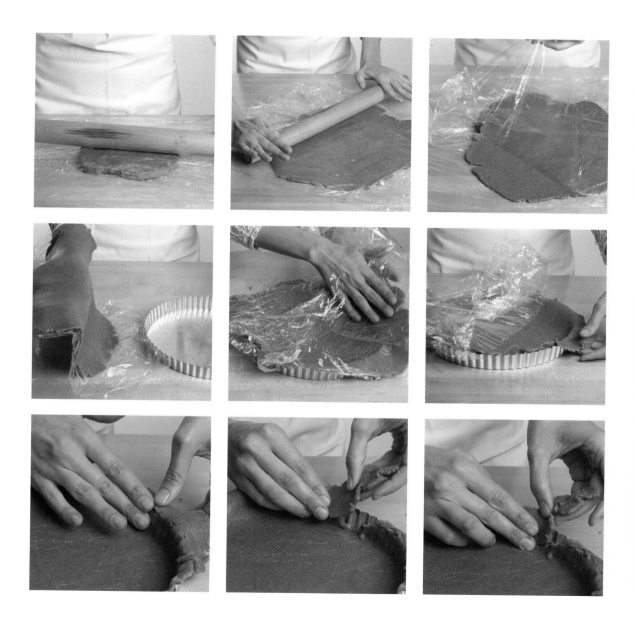

# Caramel Sauce

MAKES 1 ⅓ CUPS

PER SERVING (SCANT 3 TABLESPOONS): 130 CALORIES, 3 GRAMS FAT

1 cup sugar

¼ cup heavy cream

¼ cup nonfat milk

⅛ teaspoon salt

Caramel is easy to make at home and a delicious addition to ice cream or fresh fruit. But, heavy with sugar and cream, traditional caramel sauces can weigh down an otherwise healthy recipe. Here is a caramel with all the flavor and richness of one made with cream, but without all the fat and calories. The solution: use cream at the start to prevent the sauce from separating, then add the water and skim milk later.

MAKE AHEAD!

The completely cooled caramel can be refrigerated in an airtight container for up to 2 weeks. If the sauce separates, stir to smooth it before serving.

In a small nonreactive saucepan (stainless steel or copper works best; avoid nonstick), stir the sugar with ¼ cup water to completely moisten the sugar. Bring the mixture to a boil over medium heat, using a pastry brush dipped into cold water to brush any sugar crystals from the sides of the pan.

Once the syrup is clear, raise the heat to high and cook without stirring, swirling the pan occasionally, for 5 to 10 minutes, until the syrup is a deep caramel color. Remove the pan from the heat and carefully pour in the cream—the mixture will sputter and bubble up.

Once the hissing and bubbling subside, add another ¼ cup water. Then stir in the milk and salt, stirring vigorously to make a smooth sauce. The sauce will thicken as it cools.

Coffee-Bourbon Caramel Sauce  Dissolve 2½ teaspoons instant espresso powder in ¼ cup water and add to the sauce after the cream, in place of the ¼ cup water. Whisk in 1 teaspoon bourbon with the milk and salt.

# Simple Fudge Sauce

MAKES APPROXIMATELY ⅔ CUP

PER SERVING (GENEROUS 2 TABLESPOONS): 70 CALORIES, 4.5 GRAMS FAT
PER SERVING (SUGAR FREE): 80 CALORIES, 7 GRAMS FAT

2 ounces (⅓ cup) semisweet chocolate chips or finely chopped semisweet chocolate

¼ cup plus 1 teaspoon nonfat milk

This easy-to-prepare sauce delivers rich chocolate taste in just a few quick seconds, with considerably fewer calories and less fat than traditional sauces made with cream and butter. Serve the sauce over ice cream or with fresh fruit as a simple chocolate fondue.

Put the chocolate and the milk into a small microwave-safe bowl. Microwave on high power for 30 to 40 seconds, stopping to stir every 15 seconds, until the chocolate is completely melted and the sauce is smooth. (Alternatively, warm the chocolate and milk in a small saucepan over medium-low heat, stirring constantly, until smooth.)

**MAKE AHEAD!**

The cooled fudge sauce can be refrigerated in a covered container for up to 2 weeks. To warm the sauce, heat it gently, stirring, until warm to the touch.

**SWEET & SUGAR FREE!**

Replace the semisweet chocolate with 2 ounces (⅓ cup) chopped unsweetened chocolate and 1 tablespoon plus 2 teaspoons (6 packets) of Truvía. Bring the Truvía and milk to a boil in a small saucepan over medium-high heat; then remove from the heat and whisk in the unsweetened chocolate until it is melted and the sauce is smooth.

# Crème Anglaise

MAKES 1 ⅛ CUPS

PER SERVING (2 TABLESPOONS): 25 CALORIES, 0 GRAMS FAT

¼ cup liquid egg substitute

¼ teaspoon cornstarch

3 tablespoons sugar

1 vanilla bean

¾ cup 2% milk

MAKE AHEAD!

The sauce can be refrigerated, tightly covered, for up to 1 week in advance.

Crème anglaise was one of the first sauces I learned to make in culinary school, and to this day, it remains a personal favorite. Although the name sounds intimidating, it's just a classic vanilla sauce that is simple to prepare and makes a perfect companion for fresh berries, soufflés, cakes, and bread pudding.

In a heatproof measuring cup or a medium bowl with a pouring spout, whisk the egg substitute and cornstarch. Set aside near the stove.

Put the sugar into a small saucepan. Use a paring knife to slit the vanilla bean lengthwise and scrape the seeds into the sugar. (Reserve the pod for another use.) Whisk in the milk and cook over medium heat until it is steaming.

Pour the hot milk into the egg mixture, whisking constantly. Return the mixture to the saucepan and cook over medium heat, whisking constantly, for 1 to 2 minutes, until it coats the back of a spoon.

Strain the sauce through a fine-mesh strainer into a small bowl. Cover loosely with plastic film and refrigerate for at least 2 hours, until it is cold. Press a piece of plastic film directly against the surface of the cold sauce to prevent a skin from forming.

# Luscious Whipped Topping

MAKES APPROXIMATELY 1½ CUPS

PER SERVING (¼ CUP): 80 CALORIES, 4 GRAMS FAT

PER SERVING (SUGAR FREE): 60 CALORIES, 4 GRAMS FAT

½ cup fat-free evaporated milk

¾ teaspoon unflavored gelatin powder

⅓ cup heavy cream

2 tablespoons sugar

1 teaspoon pure vanilla extract

SWEET & SUGAR FREE!

Substitute 1½ teaspoons (2 packets) of Truvía for the sugar.

This topping has a texture similar to whipped cream, but only a fraction of the fat and calories. A hint of cream ensures real whipped cream flavor. The topping is at its best just after it is made.

Pour the evaporated milk into a small saucepan. Whisk in the gelatin, and let it stand for 3 minutes to soften. Warm the mixture over medium heat, stirring, until the milk is hot and the gelatin is completely dissolved. Do not boil.

Transfer the mixture to a medium bowl and freeze it for 10 to 15 minutes, until it is very cold and is beginning to gel around the edges.

Beat the cream, sugar, and vanilla together until the mixture holds firm peaks.

Using an electric mixer, beat the chilled evaporated milk on medium-high speed until it has the appearance of whipped cream. Use a whisk to gently fold the cream mixture into the whipped milk.

Refrigerate any leftover topping in a tightly covered container for up to 2 days; whisk to blend just before serving.

# Quick Sour Cream Whipped Topping

MAKES A GENEROUS 3 CUPS

PER SERVING (ABOUT 3 TABLESPOONS): 60 CALORIES, 4.5 GRAMS FAT

PER SERVING (SUGAR FREE): 50 CALORIES, 4.5 GRAMS FAT

¾ cup heavy cream, cold

1 cup nonfat sour cream, cold

2½ tablespoons sugar

1½ teaspoons fresh lemon juice

**SWEET & SUGAR FREE!**

Substitute 1½ teaspoons (2 packets) of Truvía for the sugar.

Even if you prefer your whipped cream on the softer side, beat the cream to firm peaks for this one—the topping will be soft and silky once the sour cream has been added.

Using an electric mixer and a chilled bowl, beat the cream on high speed until very firm peaks form; they should not droop or sag when you lift the beater. Whisk in the sour cream, sugar, and lemon juice until they are incorporated. Refrigerate, covered, for up to 2 days; rewhip before serving.

# Vanilla Ice Cream

½ cup plus 2 tablespoons sugar

1 vanilla bean

½ cup 2% milk

½ cup liquid egg substitute

1½ cups fat-free half-and-half, cold

½ teaspoon pure vanilla extract

**MAKE AHEAD!**

The ice cream mixture can be refrigerated, tightly covered, for up to 3 days before freezing it in an ice cream maker.

**SWEET & SUGAR FREE!**

Substitute ¼ cup plus ¼ teaspoon (15 packets) of Truvía for the sugar.

**Made with both vanilla bean and extract, this ice cream is the real vanilla deal! It is at its richest and creamiest the day it is made, so wait to process the mixture in your ice cream machine until just before you will serve it.**

Put the sugar into a small saucepan. Use a paring knife to slit the vanilla bean lengthwise and scrape the seeds into the sugar. Stir in the milk, then drop in the vanilla pod. Bring the mixture to a simmer over medium heat, stirring.

Put the egg substitute into a medium bowl and slowly pour in the hot milk, whisking constantly. Pour the milk and egg mixture back into the saucepan and cook over medium heat, whisking constantly, for 2 minutes, or until the mixture coats a wooden spoon.

Strain through a fine-mesh strainer into a medium bowl. Whisk in the half-and-half and the vanilla extract. Refrigerate for several hours, until the mixture is very cold.

Transfer the mixture to an ice cream maker and freeze according to the manufacturer's directions.

# Sugar-Free Sponge Cake

MAKES TWO 9-INCH LAYERS

PER SERVING (12 SERVINGS), VANILLA: 60 CALORIES, 1.5 GRAMS FAT
PER SERVING (12 SERVINGS), CHOCOLATE: 50 CALORIES, 1.5 GRAMS FAT

Nonstick pan spray

¾ cup cake flour

⅛ teaspoon salt

3 large eggs, at room temperature

4 egg whites from large eggs, at room temperature

⅔ cup (40 packets) Truvía

⅛ teaspoon cream of tartar

2 teaspoons pure vanilla extract

MAKE AHEAD!

The cooled cakes can be stored at room temperature, wrapped tightly in plastic film, for up to 1 day in advance.

Now you can have your cake and eat it, too! These cakes are as light and tender as those made with sugar. In addition to using the cake in the sugar-free substitutions throughout the book, experiment by using it in other recipes or as the basis for your own creations.

Preheat the oven to 350°F with racks in the upper and lower thirds of the oven. Line the bottoms of two 9-inch springform or 9 × 2-inch round cake pans with parchment paper. Coat the parchment and the pan sides with pan spray.

In a small bowl, sift together the flour and salt; set aside.

Using a standing mixer fitted with the whisk attachment, beat the eggs and one of the egg whites on high speed for 1 minute. Add ⅓ cup (20 packets) of Truvía and beat for 5 to 6 minutes longer, until the mixture is thick, pale, and about tripled in volume. Set aside. (Alternatively, use a handheld electric mixer.)

In a clean bowl, with clean beaters, beat the remaining 3 egg whites until foamy. Add the cream of tartar and beat just until incorporated. With the mixer running, gradually add the remaining ⅓ cup (20 packets) of Truvía, continuing to beat until the whites hold firm peaks when you lift the beaters. Add the vanilla and beat just until combined.

Sift the flour mixture over the whole-egg mixture, folding it in with a spatula in a few quick strokes. Use a rubber spatula to fold the egg whites into the batter in two parts, folding until streaky after the first addition, and just until there are no more visible white streaks after the second.

Divide the batter evenly between the prepared pans, smooth and level the tops, and bake on separate racks for 20 minutes, or until a knife inserted into the center comes out clean.

Let the cakes cool in the pans on a wire rack for 2 hours.

Run a knife around the edges of the pans to release the cakes. Invert the cakes directly onto the rack and remove the pans and parchment. Proceed according to recipe instructions for frosting and finishing.

*Sugar-Free Chocolate Sponge Cake*  Replace ¼ cup of the cake flour with ¼ cup unsweetened Dutch-processed cocoa powder and reduce the vanilla extract to 1 teaspoon.

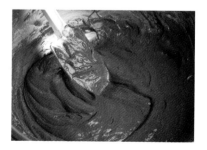

CHAPTER 2

# american classics

*For me, classic American desserts go beyond those*
that touch on our national culinary history. They also include the ones that bring back fond memories from childhood. They are the treats that originated in diners and at soda fountains—favorites like chocolate cake and peach cobbler. They include regional specialties like Boston cream pie that crept into kitchens across America right alongside the chocolate chip cookie. These recipes are the dessert equivalent of a Norman Rockwell painting.

One bite of these American classics takes me right back to the ice cream parlor in the small town where I grew up, where the scent of freshly pressed waffle cones filled the air and a pristine red-and-white checkered floor led the way to a display case speckled with candy-filled jars and giant lollipops. At the counter, thick ribbons of hot fudge snaked through every imaginable flavor of ice cream, and sundaes were piled high with whipped cream and chopped nuts.

The recipes that follow will transport you back to your sweetest child-hood memories. And since they contain a little less fat and fewer calories, you can indulge in a nostalgic moment while feeling as carefree as you did in your youth.

# PB&J Cookies

MAKES 16 COOKIES

PER COOKIE: 130 CALORIES, 6 GRAMS FAT
PER COOKIE (SUGAR FREE): 90 CALORIES, 6 GRAMS FAT

Nonstick pan spray (if not using parchment or a baking mat)

¾ cup all-purpose flour

¾ teaspoon salt

⅔ cup reduced-fat smooth peanut butter, preferably natural style

1 ounce (2 tablespoons) reduced-fat cream cheese (neufchâtel)

2 tablespoons (¼ stick) unsalted butter, softened

¼ cup granulated sugar

¼ cup (packed) dark brown sugar

3 tablespoons liquid egg substitute

½ teaspoon pure vanilla extract

About ¼ cup strawberry jam or grape jelly

You know that lone child in the cafeteria who would not touch a PB&J sandwich? That was me! After years of protest, however, I saw the light and joined the millions who delight in this all-American combination. In every restaurant where I have worked as a pastry chef, I have created some sort of peanut butter and jelly dessert. The PB&J cookie has always been the biggest hit, and, thankfully, it's not difficult to fit all that great flavor into a cookie with fewer calories. The construction of the cookies may seem a bit fussy, but it's not difficult and the finished cookies are adorable!

Preheat the oven to 350°F with a rack in the center position. Coat a baking sheet with pan spray (even if it is nonstick), or line it with parchment paper or a silicone baking mat.

In a small bowl, whisk together the flour and salt; set aside.

In a medium bowl, using an electric mixer, beat the peanut butter, cream cheese, butter, and granulated and brown sugars together on medium speed for 2 to 3 minutes, until the mixture is well blended. (If using a standing mixer, use the paddle attachment.) Add the egg substitute and vanilla and mix for 2 minutes longer. Scrape down the sides of the bowl with a rubber spatula. Add the flour mixture on low speed, beating for 1 minute, just until it is incorporated.

Set aside ⅔ cup of the dough for the cookie tops. Scoop the remaining dough into 16 equal portions and roll them between your hands to form balls. Use your thumb or index finger to press a hole about ¼ inch deep into the center of each ball, gently pinching the dough to create a well about the size of a quarter. Fill each hole with ½ to ¾ teaspoon of the jam.

recipe continues

MAKE
AHEAD!

The filled cookies can be frozen on the baking sheet, tightly wrapped with plastic film, for up to 1 week. Thaw overnight in the refrigerator before baking.

SWEET
& SUGAR
FREE!

Substitute 5 tablespoons (18 packets) of Truvía for the granulated and dark brown sugars, and use a sugar-free jam in the filling.

Roll out the reserved dough between two large pieces of plastic film until it is ⅛ inch thick. Peel off the top film and use a 1½-inch round cookie cutter to cut out 16 rounds, rerolling the scraps as needed. Use the tines of a fork to press crosshatch marks onto the flat cookie tops, dipping the fork into flour as needed to prevent sticking. If the dough becomes too soft to work with, freeze it for 5 minutes and try again.

Lay one cookie top over each of the filled cookies and press the tops and bottoms together all around the edges to seal in the jam.

Space the cookies evenly on the prepared baking sheet and bake for about 15 minutes, until the dough no longer appears wet or shiny but has not begun to brown. Halfway through the baking time, rotate the pan from front to back.

Transfer the baking sheet to a wire rack and let the cookies cool for 15 minutes. Then transfer the cookies directly to the rack and let them cool completely. Store any leftover cookies in an airtight container at room temperature for 2 to 3 days.

# Chocolate Chip Cookies

MAKES 24 COOKIES

PER COOKIE: 90 CALORIES, 3.5 GRAMS FAT

Nonstick pan spray (if not using parchment or baking mats)

1 cup minus 1 tablespoon (15 tablespoons) all-purpose flour

½ teaspoon salt

½ teaspoon baking soda

⅓ cup Browned Butter (page 24), softened

⅔ cup (packed) dark brown sugar

2 tablespoons liquid egg substitute

1 tablespoon nonfat or 1% milk

½ teaspoon pure vanilla extract

⅔ cup semisweet chocolate chips

MAKE AHEAD!

The scooped cookie dough can be stored in a resealable plastic bag and refrigerated for up to 2 weeks before baking, or frozen for up to 1 month. Bring the dough to room temperature before baking.

Chocolate chip cookies are such a quintessential childhood favorite—how could a low-fat version possibly live up to Mom's buttery cookies? Browning the butter and using brown sugar brings out every bit of flavor from these ingredients, making these cookies deceptively rich with considerably less fat. They are best enjoyed the day they are baked.

Preheat the oven to 350°F with one rack in the center position and one in the top position. Coat three baking sheets with pan spray (even if they are nonstick), or line them with parchment paper or silicone baking mats.

In a small bowl, whisk together the flour, salt, and baking soda; set aside.

In a medium bowl, using an electric mixer, beat the butter and brown sugar on medium speed for 2 minutes. (If using a standing mixer, use the paddle attachment.) Add the egg substitute, milk, and vanilla, mixing for 1 minute or until well blended. Mix in the flour mixture just until combined. Add the chocolate chips.

Scoop the dough to make 24 cookies using about 1 tablespoon each and spacing them widely, just 8 to a sheet, to allow for spreading. Press the cookies flat with the palm of your hand to slightly flatten them.

Place one baking sheet on the center oven rack and bake for 8 to 10 minutes, until the cookies are brown at the edges, rotating the pan front to back halfway through baking. Transfer the sheet to the top rack and bake for 1 minute more, until the tops of the cookies are golden.

Transfer the cookies directly to wire racks to cool. Repeat with the remaining baking sheets.

# Oatmeal-Sour Cherry Cookies

MAKES 18 COOKIES

PER COOKIE: 190 CALORIES, 7 GRAMS FAT

PER COOKIE (SUGAR FREE): 130 CALORIES, 6 GRAMS FAT

Nonstick pan spray

½ cup walnut halves or pieces

1¼ cups dried sour cherries, or ¾ cup raisins

½ cup rolled oats

⅓ cup semisweet chocolate chips

⅔ cup all-purpose flour

2 tablespoons whole wheat flour

1 teaspoon ground cinnamon

½ teaspoon baking soda

½ teaspoon baking powder

¼ teaspoon salt

6 tablespoons (¾ stick) unsalted butter, softened

¾ cup (packed) dark brown sugar

Scant ¼ cup liquid egg substitute

1 teaspoon pure vanilla extract

If you are obsessed with cookies, as I am, you will love these chewy oatmeal cookies. They are bursting with chocolate and the sweet-sour zing of tart cherries. Plumping the dried fruit in water keeps it moist and full of flavor. The secret to reducing the butter without compromising the texture is in the mixing; overmixing will make these cookies cakey rather than chewy-crisp.

Preheat the oven to 375°F with one rack in the center position and one in the top position. Coat an unrimmed baking sheet with pan spray.

Put the walnuts in a small pan and toast in the oven for 7 to 10 minutes, until you begin to smell their aroma. Let them cool for 10 minutes, then coarsely chop.

While the nuts are toasting, put the dried cherries in a small bowl and cover them completely with hot water. Let stand for 10 to 15 minutes to plump. Drain the water, and place the cherries in a medium bowl. Stir in the oats, chocolate chips, and chopped walnuts; set aside.

In a small bowl, whisk together the all-purpose and whole wheat flours, cinnamon, baking soda, baking powder, and salt; set aside.

In a medium bowl, using an electric mixer, beat the butter and brown sugar together on medium speed for 2 minutes. (If using a standing mixer, use the paddle attachment.) Add the egg substitute and vanilla, and beat for 1 minute longer. Add the flour mixture at low speed, mixing for 30 seconds. The flour will not be completely mixed in. Stir in the oat mixture with a wooden spoon just until incorporated.

recipe continues

**MAKE AHEAD!**

Scoop, flatten, and refrigerate the dough in a resealable plastic bag for up to 2 weeks, or freeze for up to 1 month. Bring the dough to room temperature before baking.

**SWEET & SUGAR FREE!**

Substitute 5 tablespoons (18 packets) of Truvía for the brown sugar. Replace the chocolate chips with an additional ¼ cup sour cherries or ⅓ cup sugar-free chocolate chips.

Using a small scoop or a spoon, scoop out 18 cookies, using about 2 tablespoons each, onto the prepared baking sheet, spacing them several inches apart for spreading. Gently flatten the cookies with the palm of your hand to a ¼- to ½-inch thickness. Bake on the center rack for 8 minutes. Then transfer the sheet to the top rack and bake for another 1 to 2 minutes, just until the edges and tops of the cookies are beginning to brown.

Transfer the cookies directly to a wire rack and let them cool for 10 to 15 minutes. Serve slightly warm, or store in an airtight container at room temperature for up to 2 days.

# Lemon Bars

## crust

Nonstick pan spray

¼ cup Browned Butter (page 24), softened

¾ ounce (1½ tablespoons) reduced-fat cream cheese (neufchâtel), preferably Kraft brand

2 teaspoons non-hydrogenated vegetable shortening, such as Spectrum brand

¼ cup powdered sugar

1 tablespoon liquid egg substitute

1 teaspoon pure vanilla extract

1 cup all-purpose flour

## filling

1 tablespoon finely grated lemon zest

¾ cup strained fresh lemon juice (from 3 to 4 lemons)

¼ cup strained fresh orange juice (from 1 to 2 oranges)

¾ cup liquid egg substitute

1⅔ cups granulated sugar

½ cup plus 1 tablespoon all-purpose flour

⅛ teaspoon salt

2 large eggs

Powdered sugar, for garnish (optional)

When I made these rich-tasting bars during *Food Network Challenge*'s mystery cookies challenge, the judges could not believe they were low-fat. Browning the butter is the key—it makes the crumbly cookie crust taste deceptively buttery. The addition of orange juice to the filling gets the sweet-tart balance just right with less sugar. If you wish to dust the tops with powdered sugar, do so just before serving to keep it from disappearing into the bars.

To make the crust: Coat a 9-inch square baking pan with pan spray.

In a medium bowl, using an electric mixer on medium speed, mix the butter, cream cheese, shortening, and powdered sugar together for 5 to 6 minutes, until the mixture is completely smooth. (If using a standing mixer, use the paddle attachment.) Add the egg substitute and vanilla, and mix for another 2 minutes. Scrape down the sides of the bowl with a spatula. Then add the flour and mix for an additional 5 minutes.

Press the dough evenly into the prepared pan, covering the bottom and about ¼ inch up the sides. (If the dough becomes sticky, cover it with a piece of plastic film and continue to press with your fingertips or the flat bottom of a glass; remove the film before baking.) Place the pan in the freezer and chill for 10 to 15 minutes, until the dough is firm to the touch.

Meanwhile, preheat the oven to 350°F with one rack in the upper third of the oven and another rack in the center position.

recipe continues

Prick the dough all over with a fork. Bake it on the center oven rack for 20 minutes. Then move the pan to the upper rack, rotating the pan from front to back, and bake for another 10 minutes, or until the crust is a deep golden brown all over.

*To make the filling:* In a medium bowl, whisk together the lemon zest, lemon and orange juices, and egg substitute; set aside.

In a large bowl, whisk together the sugar, flour, and salt until well combined. Whisk in the juice mixture, then the eggs, continuing to whisk for 1 to 2 minutes longer, until the mixture is completely free of lumps.

*To finish:* Remove the crust from the oven, stir the filling once more, and then immediately pour it into the crust. Loosely drape a sheet of aluminum foil over the top and return the pan to the center rack of the oven. Bake for 35 to 40 minutes, until the filling is set.

Transfer the pan to a wire rack and leave it for several hours, until the pan is cool to the touch. Then refrigerate the pan for several hours for easiest cutting.

*To serve:* Cut into 4 strips in one direction, then 4 in the other, to make 16 bars. Dust the tops of the bars with powdered sugar just before serving, if desired.

Refrigerate any leftover bars, tightly wrapped, for up to 4 days, or freeze them for up to 2 weeks; thaw frozen bars overnight in the refrigerator before serving.

# Whoopie Pies

PER PIE: 170 CALORIES, 6 GRAMS FAT

Nonstick pan spray (if not using parchment or baking mats)

1⅔ cups all-purpose flour

⅓ cup whole wheat flour

½ cup good-quality unsweetened cocoa powder, natural or Dutch-processed

1¼ teaspoons baking soda

1 teaspoon salt

1 cup plain nonfat Greek-style yogurt

¼ cup low-fat buttermilk

½ teaspoon pure vanilla extract

⅔ cup (packed) dark brown sugar

¼ cup (½ stick) unsalted butter, softened

2 teaspoons non-hydrogenated shortening, such as Spectrum brand

3 tablespoons liquid egg substitute

1 cup Vanilla Marshmallow (page 116) or store-bought marshmallow creme

I was eight years old when I tasted my first whoopie pie at a roller-skating rink. Staring back across the counter, alongside the hot dogs and cotton candy, were little chocolate cakes filled with fluffy white cream, looking nothing like any pie I had ever seen. As I took a bite, my doubts quickly faded. Either natural or Dutch-processed cocoa works well in this recipe; more important is to use a good-quality cocoa for the best flavor.

The Vanilla Marshmallow recipe (see page 116) makes the perfect filling for these pies. Use the marshmallow straight from the bowl after whipping, rather than spreading it into a pan. (The remaining mixture can be made into marshmallows following the recipe instructions.)

Preheat the oven to 350°F with one rack in the bottom third and another in the top third of the oven. Coat two 17 × 12-inch rimmed baking sheets with pan spray (even if they are nonstick), or line them with silicone baking mats or parchment paper.

In a medium bowl, whisk together the all-purpose and whole wheat flours, cocoa powder, baking soda, and salt; set aside. In another medium bowl, whisk together the yogurt, buttermilk, and vanilla until the mixture is smooth.

In a large bowl, using an electric mixer, beat the brown sugar, butter, and shortening together on medium-high speed for 6 to 7 minutes, until the mixture is light and fluffy. (If using a standing mixer, use the paddle attachment.) Add the egg substitute and beat on medium for 2 minutes longer. Add one-third of the flour mixture and beat on low

recipe continues

MAKE
AHEAD!

The batter for the pies can be
made up to 24 hours ahead and
refrigerated, tightly covered,
before scooping and baking them.

speed for 1 minute. Scrape the bowl down, add half of the yogurt
mixture, and beat on low speed for 1 minute. Repeat this process,
scraping the bowl down and beating for 1 minute, as you add half of
the remaining flour, then all of the remaining yogurt, and finally all
of the remaining flour.

Use a scoop or a large spoon to make 28 mounds on the prepared
baking sheets, using 1½ tablespoons of the batter for each mound and
spacing them 2 inches apart. (To make the smoothest cakes, coat a
small ice cream scoop with pan spray or oil, or coat your hands and
use them to shape the mounds into smooth domes.)

Bake the cakes for 12 to 14 minutes, until a skewer inserted into the
center of a cake comes out with just a few sticky crumbs stuck to it.
Halfway through the baking time, rotate the pans from top to bottom
and front to back.

Transfer the pans to a wire rack to cool, about 1 hour.

To serve: Spoon a generous tablespoon of marshmallow topping onto
the flat side of one cake and press a second cake over the filling.
Repeat with the remaining cakes and filling. Let the filled pies set for
10 minutes before serving.

Store any leftover pies, filled or unfilled, in a resealable plastic bag at
room temperature for up to 3 days. If using store-bought topping, serve
the pies within 4 hours of filling them.

# Red Velvet Cupcakes

## cupcakes

1½ cups cake flour

1 tablespoon unsweetened Dutch-processed cocoa powder

1½ teaspoons baking powder

½ teaspoon salt

½ cup low-fat buttermilk

⅓ cup canola oil

2 tablespoons finely grated raw beet

1½ tablespoons natural red food coloring

2 large eggs

2 egg whites from large eggs

1 cup granulated sugar

Red velvet cake has been around since the 1920s, its signature color ranging from bright to brownish red. I use a natural red dye (found in health food and gourmet food stores) to color these cupcakes, with beet and cocoa added to boost both color and moisture. The traditional creamy white frosting is made with milk and flour, but I think cream cheese gives the best flavor and texture. While many cakes suffer under refrigeration, these remain moist and the frosting soft and luscious.

To make the cupcakes: Preheat the oven to 350°F with a rack in the center position. Line 16 muffin cups with cupcake liners.

Sift the flour, cocoa powder, baking powder, and salt into a small bowl. Sift a second time to remove any lumps. In another small bowl, whisk together the buttermilk, oil, beet, and food coloring. Set the bowls aside.

In a large bowl, using an electric mixer, beat the eggs and egg whites on high speed until they are foamy. Gradually add the sugar and continue to beat for about 6 minutes longer, or until the mixture is thick and pale yellow. Use a spatula to gently fold the flour mixture into the eggs, then fold in the buttermilk mixture.

Divide the batter evenly among the prepared muffin cups and bake for 15 minutes, or until a wooden skewer inserted in the center of a cupcake comes out clean. Transfer the cupcakes in their liners to a wire rack to cool for at least 2 hours before frosting.

recipe continues

## frosting

6 ounces (¾ cup) reduced-fat
    cream cheese (neufchâtel)

¾ cup powdered sugar

1 vanilla bean, or 1 teaspoon pure
    vanilla extract

MAKE AHEAD!

The frosting can be made up to 1
week ahead and refrigerated,
tightly covered, before frosting the
cupcakes.

**To make the frosting:** Put the cream cheese into a medium bowl and sift in the powdered sugar. Use a paring knife to slit the vanilla bean lengthwise and scrape the seeds into the bowl, or add the vanilla extract. Beat with an electric mixer on medium speed until the frosting is completely smooth. (If using a standing mixer, use the paddle attachment.)

**To finish:** Frost the cupcakes with a small icing spatula.

Refrigerate any leftover cupcakes in an airtight container at room temperature for up to 3 days.

# Peach Cobbler

2 ounces (¼ cup) Kraft reduced-fat cream cheese (neufchâtel), cut into ½-inch cubes

2 tablespoons (¼ stick) unsalted butter, cut into ½-inch cubes

Nonstick pan spray

## filling

2½ pounds (about 6 small) yellow peaches

1 tablespoon fresh lemon juice

½ cup sugar

1½ tablespoons cornstarch

⅛ teaspoon ground ginger

¼ vanilla bean

## biscuits

2 cups cake flour or all-purpose flour

2 teaspoons baking powder

1 teaspoon sugar

½ teaspoon salt

1 cup low-fat buttermilk, cold (if using all-purpose flour, increase the buttermilk by 1 tablespoon)

Vanilla Ice Cream (page 37) or Dreyer's Slow Churned Vanilla Ice Cream, for serving (optional)

Fruit cobbler is as American as apple pie—and you don't even have to roll out pastry! For cobbler, I like the delicate, cakey biscuits that come from using cake flour. If you prefer a more traditional (breakfast-type) biscuit, substitute an equal amount of all-purpose flour for the cake flour. Either makes a superlative cobbler filled with soft, sweet fruit.

Place the cream cheese and butter cubes in a single layer on a plate, and freeze for 20 minutes, or until firm to the touch but not frozen through.

Meanwhile, preheat the oven to 425°F with one rack in the center position and a second rack in the lower third of the oven. Coat a 9½ × 2½-inch pie pan with pan spray. Bring a large pot of water to a boil.

To make the filling: Cut a small "X" in the bottom of each peach with a paring knife. Carefully drop the peaches into the boiling water and blanch for 3 to 5 minutes, using the shorter time if the fruit is very ripe. The peaches are ready when the skin begins to curl where you made the "X."

Use a slotted spoon to carefully transfer the peaches, one by one, to a colander set in the sink. Rinse the peaches under cool running water. Use your fingers or a paring knife to peel and discard the skin from the peaches. Cut the peaches into ½-inch-thick slices, transferring them to a large bowl as you go. Add the lemon juice and toss to coat the fruit.

**SWEET & SUGAR FREE!**

Substitute ¼ cup (15 packets) of Truvía for the sugar in the filling. Omit the sugar in the biscuits.

In a small bowl, stir together the sugar, cornstarch, and ginger. Use a paring knife to slit the vanilla bean lengthwise and scrape the seeds into the sugar mixture. Add the sugar mixture to the peaches and stir gently until they are thoroughly and evenly coated. Transfer the peaches and all of their juices to the prepared pan.

*To make the biscuits:* In a medium bowl, whisk together the flour, baking powder, sugar, and salt. Cut in the cold cream cheese and butter with a fork or a pastry cutter until they are in small pieces ranging from the size of oat flakes to peas. (Alternatively, use a standing mixer with the paddle attachment on low speed to mix in the cream cheese and butter.) Stir in the buttermilk, mixing just long enough to make a soft dough.

*To finish:* Dollop the dough in large spoonfuls (about ⅓ cup each) over the peaches in the pie pan to make 10 to 12 biscuits.

Bake on the center oven rack for 20 minutes. Then rotate the pan, transfer it to the lower rack, and bake for another 15 minutes, or until the biscuits are golden and the peaches are tender when you pierce them with a fork. Let cool for 20 minutes.

*To serve:* Scoop out the cobbler into bowls, including a biscuit with each serving. Top with ice cream, if desired.

Store any leftovers at room temperature, tightly covered, for up to 2 days.

# Apple Pandowdy

PER SERVING: 230 CALORIES, 6 GRAMS FAT

PER SERVING (SUGAR FREE): 190 CALORIES, 6 GRAMS FAT

Dough for 1 Cream Cheese Pie Crust (page 26)

Oil or nonstick pan spray

5 large Fuji or Granny Smith apples, peeled, cored, and cut into ¼-inch-thick slices

1 tablespoon fresh lemon juice

1½ teaspoons finely grated orange zest

3 tablespoons fresh orange juice

2 tablespoons dark rum or brandy

1 tablespoon honey

⅓ cup granulated sugar

¼ cup (packed) dark brown sugar

1 tablespoon plus 1 teaspoon cornstarch

1 teaspoon ground cinnamon

½ teaspoon ground ginger

⅛ teaspoon salt

¼ cup pitted dates, chopped, or ¼ cup dark raisins

¼ cup chopped toasted walnuts

Vanilla Ice Cream (page 37) or Dreyer's Slow Churned Vanilla Ice Cream, for serving (optional)

My Greek grandparents owned a successful restaurant called the College Inn Café in Manhattan, Kansas, that served everything from steaks and burgers to chop suey and, of course, apple pie! My *pappou* Andreas was more of a chef than a baker, so he called his brother, Pete, for his apple pandowdy recipe, which sold out daily at Pete's restaurants. It had only a top crust, which kept the filling juicy without a bottom crust getting soggy. Pappou's only problem was making the staff save the pandowdy for the customers!

Roll out the pie crust dough as described on page 000, leave it between the sheets of plastic film, and refrigerate it for at least 30 minutes.

Preheat the oven to 425°F with one rack in the center position and another in the bottom third of the oven. Oil or lightly spray a 10 × 2- to 2½-inch pie pan.

Put the apples in a large bowl. Add the lemon juice, orange zest and juice, rum, honey, and 1 tablespoon water. Stir to evenly coat the fruit. In a small bowl, stir together the granulated and brown sugars, cornstarch, cinnamon, ginger, and salt. Add the sugar mixture to the apples and stir to coat them evenly. Stir in the dates and walnuts. Transfer the apple mixture to the prepared pie pan.

Use a pastry wheel or a sharp knife to cut the chilled crust into 2-inch squares. Distribute the squares evenly over the apples in the pan, overlapping them slightly and leaving a few pieces of apple peeking through.

recipe continues

Bake the pandowdy on the center oven rack for 20 minutes. Then move the pan to the lower rack and bake for an additional 15 to 20 minutes, until the crust is golden and the juices are bubbling. Let it cool for 20 minutes before serving.

*To serve:* Spoon the pandowdy into bowls and top with a scoop of ice cream, if desired.

Cover any leftover pandowdy with plastic film or foil and store it at room temperature for 2 to 3 days. Enjoy at room temperature or warmed in the oven.

# Boston Cream Pie

SERVES 12

PER SERVING: 270 CALORIES, 9 GRAMS FAT
PER SERVING (SUGAR FREE): 150 CALORIES, 7.5 GRAMS FAT

## cake

Nonstick pan spray

1 cup cake flour

1 teaspoon baking powder

¼ teaspoon salt

⅓ cup low-fat buttermilk

¼ cup canola oil

½ teaspoon pure vanilla extract

2 large eggs, at room temperature

2 egg whites from large eggs,
    at room temperature

⅔ cup sugar

**MAKE AHEAD!**

The custard can be made a day ahead and refrigerated; press plastic film directly onto the surface of the cooled custard to prevent a skin from forming. The glaze can be made several days ahead and refrigerated, covered, until you are ready to finish the cake.

My mother and I rarely agree on a dessert to share, but Boston Cream Pie is one we can always enjoy together. She dives straight into the center, while I go for the chocolate glaze. In short, this is the perfect cake to satisfy vanilla- and chocolate-lovers alike. The coffee extract gives the glaze an extra-chocolatey finish.

**To make the cake:** Preheat the oven to 350°F with a rack in the center position. Coat a 9-inch springform or other round cake pan with pan spray.

Sift the flour, baking powder, and salt into a small bowl. In another small bowl, whisk together the buttermilk, oil, and vanilla. Set the bowls aside.

In a large bowl, use an electric mixer to beat the eggs and egg whites on high speed for 1 minute. With the mixer running, gradually add the sugar, beating for about 8 minutes altogether, until the mixture is thick and pale. Sift the flour mixture over the egg mixture and fold it in with a rubber spatula. Gently fold in the buttermilk mixture just until it is incorporated.

Spread the batter in the prepared pan and bake for 30 minutes, until the top is golden and a toothpick inserted into the center comes out clean. Transfer the pan to a wire rack to cool.

recipe continues

## custard

⅔ cup liquid egg substitute

2 tablespoons cornstarch

⅛ teaspoon salt

½ cup sugar

½ vanilla bean

1½ cups 2% milk

## glaze

½ cup semisweet chocolate chips

2 tablespoons light corn syrup

2 teaspoons coffee extract
   or strong freshly brewed
   espresso (optional)

SWEET & SUGAR FREE!

Substitute Sugar-Free Sponge Cake (page 38) for the cake. For the custard, substitute 3½ table-spoons (13 packets) of Truvía for the sugar. For the glaze, substitute 4 ounces chopped unsweetened chocolate and 3 tablespoons plus ¾ teaspoon (12 packets) of Truvía for the chocolate chips, and 2 tablespoons agave nectar for the corn syrup. Heat the Truvía, agave, and ⅓ cup water until the crystals dissolve. Remove from the heat and whisk in the chocolate until melted. Finish as described.

**To make the custard:** Set a fine-mesh strainer over a medium bowl near the stove. In a large bowl, whisk together the egg substitute, cornstarch, and salt. Set aside.

Put the sugar in a medium saucepan. Use a paring knife to slit the vanilla bean lengthwise and scrape the seeds into the sugar; drop in the pod. Whisk in the milk. Bring the mixture to a simmer over medium heat, stirring.

Pour the hot milk into the egg mixture in a slow stream, whisking constantly. Return the mixture to the saucepan and cook over medium-low heat, stirring constantly, for 4 to 5 minutes, until it coats the back of a spoon. Immediately pour the mixture through the sieve into the bowl. Cover loosely with plastic film and refrigerate until it is cold, 1 to 2 hours.

**To make the glaze:** Combine the chocolate chips, corn syrup, and ⅓ cup water in a small saucepan, and warm over medium-low heat until you can stir the mixture smooth. Add the coffee, if using. Cover loosely with plastic film and refrigerate until the glaze thickens, about 2 hours.

**To finish:** Cut the cake in half horizontally to form 2 layers. Place the bottom half on a serving platter and spread the custard over it. Top with the second cake layer. Pour and spread the chocolate glaze over the cake, allowing some to run down the sides. (If needed, gently warm the glaze until it is pourable.)

**To serve:** Immediately after glazing, cut the cake into 12 wedges.

Refrigerate any leftover cake, covering it lightly with plastic film after the glaze has set, for up to 3 days.

# Sour Cherry Pie

PER SERVING: 230 CALORIES, 4.5 GRAMS FAT

PER SERVING (SUGAR FREE): 180 CALORIES, 4.5 GRAMS FAT

Nonstick pan spray

¾ cup sugar

¼ cup plus 1 teaspoon cornstarch

⅛ teaspoon salt

6 cups pitted sour cherries, at room temperature, or three 14.5-ounce cans pitted sour cherries, drained

½ teaspoon pure almond extract

Cream Cheese Pie Crust (page 26) for a lattice-top pie, unbaked, crust chilled

Vanilla Ice Cream (page 37) or Dreyer's Slow Churned Vanilla Ice Cream, for serving (optional)

SWEET & SUGAR FREE!

Substitute 7½ tablespoons (30 packets) of Truvía for the sugar in the filling, and prepare the Cream Cheese Pie Crust (page 26) without sugar.

I always look forward to the short sour cherry season (late June through early July), when I use the tangy fruit in compotes and pies. When fresh cherries are not available, you can make a perfectly respectable pie using canned or jarred tart cherries packed in water. To me, cherry pie absolutely must sport a lattice crust and should be served with vanilla ice cream.

Preheat the oven to 425°F with one rack in the center position and another in the lower third. Coat a 9 × 2½-inch pie pan with pan spray.

In a small bowl, stir together the sugar, cornstarch, and salt. Put the cherries in a large bowl, and add the almond extract along with the sugar mixture. Stir with a large spoon until the fruit is evenly coated. Pour the filling into the chilled pie crust.

Evenly space 5 pastry strips across the top of the pie in one direction. Lay the remaining 5 strips at an angle across the first set of strips to create a lattice. Trim the strips to the edges of the pan, and press the ends of the strips firmly against the bottom crust to seal.

Bake the pie on the center oven rack for 20 minutes. Then transfer it to the lower rack, rotating the pan front to back. Bake for another 25 to 30 minutes, until the crust is golden and the fruit is bubbling. If the crust browns too quickly, drape foil over the pie to complete the baking. Don't be concerned if the juices appear liquidy; they will be reabsorbed by the cherries as the pie cools. Let the pie cool for at least 30 minutes.

To serve: Cut the pie into 12 wedges. Serve warm or at room temperature, with vanilla ice cream, if desired.

Store leftovers at room temperature, covered tightly with foil, for 2 days.

# Warm Blueberry Crisp

SERVES 6

PER SERVING: 240 CALORIES, 6 GRAMS FAT
PER SERVING (SUGAR FREE): 150 CALORIES, 6 GRAMS FAT

## topping

¼ cup (½ stick) unsalted butter, cut into ¼-inch cubes

1½ ounces (3 tablespoons) reduced-fat cream cheese (neufchâtel), preferably Kraft brand, cut into ½-inch cubes

1 cup all-purpose flour

⅓ cup (packed) dark brown sugar

1 teaspoon pure vanilla extract

1 teaspoon finely grated lemon zest

¼ teaspoon ground cinnamon

¼ teaspoon ground ginger

¼ teaspoon ground nutmeg

¼ teaspoon salt

MAKE AHEAD!

Freeze the unbaked topping in a resealable plastic bag for up to 3 weeks. The topping can also be baked separately on a baking sheet at 375°F for 15 to 20 minutes, stirring occasionally, until golden and crispy. Store the baked topping in an airtight container at room temperature for up to 3 days.

An alluring blend of spices and a buttery crunch make this crisp one of my favorite comfort foods. The recipe makes more topping than is needed here—enjoy the leftovers for snacking or as a crunchy topping for yogurt or ice cream. I like to double the topping and freeze half, unbaked, to have on hand when unexpected company shows up. Sprinkle the frozen topping over the fruit filling and bake until golden and bubbling hot.

To make the topping: Arrange the butter and cream cheese cubes in a single layer on a baking sheet and freeze until firm to the touch but not frozen through, about 20 minutes.

In a medium bowl, combine the flour, brown sugar, vanilla, lemon zest, cinnamon, ginger, nutmeg, and salt. Cut in the cold butter and cream cheese, using a fork or a pastry cutter, until they are in small pebble-size pieces. (Alternatively, use a standing mixer fitted with the paddle attachment on low speed to mix in the butter and cream cheese.)

Freeze the topping mixture for at least 15 minutes.

About 20 minutes before baking, preheat the oven to 375°F with a rack in the center position.

*recipe continues*

## filling

¼ cup granulated sugar

¼ vanilla bean

½ teaspoon finely grated lemon zest

1 tablespoon all-purpose flour

1½ pints (3 cups) blueberries

1 teaspoon fresh lemon juice

1½ cups Vanilla Ice Cream (page 37) or Dreyer's Slow Churned Vanilla Ice Cream, for serving (optional)

SWEET & SUGAR FREE!

Substitute ½ cup plus 3½ tablespoons (37 packets) of Truvía for the brown sugar in the topping and 2 tablespoons plus 2 teaspoons (10 packets) of Truvía for the granulated sugar in the filling. Spread the topping on a baking sheet. Fill the ramekins with the fruit and drape a sheet of foil over them. Bake the topping for 25 minutes, or until golden, stirring occasionally. Bake the ramekins for 25 minutes, or until bubbly. To serve, sprinkle ⅓ cup of the topping over the warm fruit in each ramekin.

To make the filling: Put the sugar in a small bowl. Use a paring knife to slit the vanilla bean lengthwise and scrape the seeds into the sugar, rubbing them in with your fingertips. Stir in the lemon zest and flour. In a medium bowl, toss the berries with the lemon juice. Sprinkle the sugar mixture over the berries and toss to coat.

To finish: Divide the berries among six 4- to 6-ounce ramekins or custard cups, and top each with ⅓ cup of the topping. Bake for about 25 minutes, until the topping is golden and the berry juices are bubbling up.

To serve: Serve warm, topped with ice cream, if desired.

# Old-Fashioned Fudge Cake

SERVES 16

PER SERVING: 280 CALORIES, 12 GRAMS FAT

## cake

Nonstick pan spray

1¾ cups all-purpose flour, plus more for coating the pan

1½ cups granulated sugar

1 cup unsweetened Dutch-processed cocoa powder

1 teaspoon baking powder

1 teaspoon baking soda

½ teaspoon fine sea salt

1¼ cups low-fat buttermilk

1 cup plain nonfat Greek-style yogurt

4 egg whites from large eggs, or ¾ cup liquid egg whites

1 tablespoon extra virgin olive oil

⅔ cup (loosely packed) finely grated beets

This cake is similar to one I made on *Top Chef* that was also featured in *Food & Wine* magazine. In this version, a secret ingredient adds moisture and complements the chocolate's earthy flavor: grated beets! Unless you tell your guests, they will be none the wiser—the beets practically melt into the cake as it bakes.

To make the cake: Preheat the oven to 350°F with a rack in the center position. Coat a 10-inch round cake pan with pan spray and coat it lightly with flour, knocking out the excess.

In a small bowl, whisk together the flour, sugar, cocoa powder, baking powder, baking soda, and salt. In a large bowl, whisk the buttermilk, yogurt, egg whites, and olive oil together until the mixture is smooth. Stir in the beets, then the flour mixture, just until incorporated.

Transfer the batter to the prepared pan and bake for about 40 minutes, until the cake is slightly domed in the center and a toothpick inserted near the center comes out clean. Transfer the pan to a wire rack to cool for 20 minutes. Then run a knife around the edge and invert the cake directly onto the rack; leave it for about 1 hour longer to cool completely.

*recipe continues*

## frosting

8 ounces (1 cup) reduced-fat cream cheese (neufchâtel)

¼ cup (½ stick) unsalted butter, softened

2 cups powdered sugar

6 tablespoons unsweetened Dutch-processed cocoa powder

½ teaspoon pure vanilla extract

2 teaspoons nonfat milk

**To make the frosting:** Using a standing mixer fitted with the paddle attachment, beat the cream cheese and butter on medium speed for about 1 minute, until the mixture is smooth. Sift in the powdered sugar and cocoa powder and continue to mix, starting on low and increasing to medium speed as the sugar is incorporated, until the frosting is completely smooth. Add the vanilla and milk on low speed, mixing until incorporated. (Alternatively, use a handheld electric mixer.)

**To finish:** Use an offset spatula to frost the top of the cake first, starting at the center and pushing the frosting out to the sides. Frost the sides.

**To serve:** Cut the cake into 16 wedges.

Refrigerate any leftover cake, covered, for up to 2 days.

# Coconut Cake

## cake

Nonstick pan spray

1 cup cake flour

1 teaspoon baking powder

¼ teaspoon salt

⅓ cup 2% milk

¼ cup canola oil

1 teaspoon natural coconut
    extract, or ½ teaspoon
    artificial coconut extract

2 large eggs, at room temperature

4 egg whites from large eggs,
    at room temperature

½ cup plus 2 tablespoons sugar

Pinch of cream of tartar (optional)

MAKE AHEAD!

The custard can be made up to
2 days ahead and refrigerated;
press plastic film directly onto the
surface of the cooled custard to
prevent a skin from forming.

This classic southern cake should be delicate and moist, with a creamy filling and a fluffy topping. Like a southern belle, it's so dainty and ladylike, you almost hate to dig in and ruin the lovely cake. But, please, don't let that stop you.

To make the cake: Preheat the oven to 350°F with a rack in the center position. Coat a 9-inch springform or round cake pan with pan spray.

Sift the flour, baking powder, and salt into a small bowl. Sift the mixture again into a second small bowl, then a third time back into the original bowl. In a medium bowl, whisk together the milk, oil, and coconut extract. Set the bowls aside.

In a large bowl, using an electric mixer, beat the eggs and 2 of the egg whites on high speed for 1 minute. Gradually add the ½ cup sugar, beating for 5 minutes, until the mixture is thick and pale. Use a rubber spatula to gently fold in the sifted flour mixture. Fold in the milk mixture just until it is incorporated.

In a clean bowl with clean beaters, beat the remaining 2 egg whites on high speed until they are foamy. Add the cream of tartar, if using. Beat for 1 to 2 minutes longer while slowly adding the 2 tablespoons sugar, until the meringue forms a curl that folds over like soft-serve ice cream when you lift the beaters.

recipe continues

## coconut custard

⅔ cup liquid egg substitute

2 tablespoons cornstarch

⅛ teaspoon salt

1½ cups 2% milk

½ cup sugar

½ teaspoon natural coconut
extract, or ¼ teaspoon
artificial coconut extract

¼ cup sweetened flake coconut,
toasted

Use a rubber spatula to fold the meringue into the batter in two parts, folding just until there are no more visible streaks after each addition. Spread the batter into the prepared pan and bake for 30 minutes, or until the top is golden and a toothpick inserted into the center comes out clean.

Let the cake cool in the pan on a wire rack for 30 minutes. Then release the cake from the pan and transfer it directly to the rack to finish cooling.

To make the custard: Set a fine-mesh strainer over a medium bowl near the stove. In a large bowl, whisk together the egg substitute, cornstarch, and salt. Set aside.

In a small saucepan, whisk together the milk and sugar as you bring the mixture to a simmer over medium heat. Pour the hot milk into the egg mixture in a slow stream, whisking constantly. Return the mixture to the saucepan and cook over medium-low heat, stirring constantly, for 4 to 5 minutes, until the custard coats the back of a spoon.

Immediately pour the custard through the sieve into the bowl. Whisk in the coconut extract and the toasted coconut. Cover the bowl loosely with plastic film and refrigerate for 1 to 2 hours, until cold.

## frosting

²⁄₃ cup sugar

1 tablespoon light corn syrup

3 egg whites from large eggs,
    at room temperature

½ teaspoon natural coconut
    extract, or ¼ teaspoon
    artificial coconut extract

Pinch of salt

¾ cup sweetened flake coconut
    (untoasted), for garnish

**To make the frosting:** In a small saucepan, stir the sugar with the corn syrup and ¼ cup water to moisten the sugar. Bring the mixture to a boil over medium heat and boil for 2 minutes, stirring. As the syrup cooks, use a pastry brush dipped into cold water to brush any sugar crystals from the sides of the pan.

Using a standing mixer fitted with the whisk attachment, beat the egg whites on high speed until they turn thick and foamy. (Alternatively, use a handheld electric mixer.) With the mixer running, pour in the hot sugar syrup in a slow, steady stream, aiming it between the lip of the bowl and the beater. Once all the syrup has been added, beat for 5 minutes longer, until the bottom of the bowl feels slightly warm to the touch. Add the coconut extract and salt on low speed; then increase the speed to medium for 2 minutes longer.

**To finish:** Cut the cake in half horizontally to form 2 layers. Place the bottom half on a serving platter and spread the custard evenly over the cake. Place the top half over the custard. Use a rubber spatula to scrape all of the frosting onto the top of the cake, then use a flat metal spatula to spread the frosting over the top and sides. Sprinkle half of the untoasted coconut over the top of the cake, and use your hands to press the remaining coconut onto the sides.

**To serve:** Dip a knife into hot water and wipe it dry before cutting the cake into 12 pieces.

Refrigerate any leftover cake, tightly wrapped in plastic film, for up to 2 days.

# Strawberry Shortcakes with Sour Cream Whipped Topping

SERVES 9

PER SERVING: 290 CALORIES, 12 GRAMS FAT
PER SERVING (SUGAR FREE): 245 CALORIES, 12 GRAMS FAT

## shortcakes

2 ounces (¼ cup) Kraft reduced-fat cream cheese (neufchâtel), cold, cut into ½-inch cubes

2 tablespoons (¼ stick) unsalted butter, cold, cut into ½-inch cubes

Nonstick pan spray (if not using parchment or a baking mat)

2 cups all-purpose flour

2 teaspoons baking powder

1 teaspoon granulated sugar

½ teaspoon salt

1 cup plus 1 tablespoon low-fat buttermilk, cold

MAKE AHEAD!

The berries can be prepared and refrigerated, covered, up to 4 hours in advance. The whipped topping is best served within 3 hours of making it but can be refrigerated, tightly covered, for up to 24 hours; stir smooth before serving.

In these shortcakes, reduced-fat cream cheese replaces some of the butter used to make a traditional biscuit, leaving them with all the charm but only half the fat and calories. A good-quality dense reduced-fat cream cheese such as Kraft produces the flakiest biscuits; avoid brands that feel wet or gummy when you unwrap them. The topping is rich and creamy with less than half the fat of whipped cream thanks to nonfat sour cream, which along with the lemon juice adds a welcome tangy note. I like to serve any leftover biscuits for breakfast, split, toasted, and spread with jam.

To make the shortcakes: Arrange the cream cheese and butter cubes in a single layer on a baking sheet and freeze until they are firm to the touch but not frozen through, about 20 minutes.

Meanwhile, preheat the oven to 450°F with a rack in the center position. Coat a baking sheet with pan spray (even if it is nonstick), or line it with parchment paper or a silicone baking mat.

In a medium bowl, combine the flour, baking powder, sugar, and salt. Cut in the cold cream cheese and butter, using a fork or a pastry cutter, until they form small pieces ranging from the size of oat flakes to peas. (Alternatively, use a standing mixer fitted with the paddle attachment on low speed to mix in the butter and cream cheese.) Stir in the buttermilk, mixing just long enough to make a soft dough.

recipe continues

### strawberries

2 pints strawberries, hulled and
quartered

4 to 5 tablespoons granulated
sugar

2 teaspoons fresh lemon juice

Quick Sour Cream Whipped
Topping (page 36)

Powdered sugar, to finish
(optional)

SWEET
& SUGAR
FREE!

For the shortcakes, omit the
teaspoon of sugar. For the
strawberries, substitute 1 to
1¾ tablespoons (4 to 5 packets)
of Truvía for the sugar, to taste.
Use the sugar-free version of the
Quick Sour Cream Whipped
Topping (page 36).

Transfer the dough to a lightly floured surface, kneading gently just once or twice to bring it together. Roll or pat the dough into an approximately 7-inch square, about 1 inch thick. Use a sharp knife to cut the dough into 3 strips one way, then 3 strips the other way, to make 9 squares. Place the biscuits on the prepared baking sheet and bake for 12 to 15 minutes, until they are golden.

Transfer the baking sheet to a wire rack and let the biscuits cool completely, about 1 hour.

To prepare the berries: Put the strawberries in a medium bowl, and add the sugar and lemon juice. (Use the larger amount of sugar if the berries are very tart.) Stir for about 1 minute, until the berries begin to release their juices.

To serve: Split open the cooled biscuits and place a bottom half on each dessert plate. Spoon the berries and their juices over the biscuits and top each with ⅓ cup of the whipped topping, then a biscuit top. Lightly sift powdered sugar over the top of the shortcakes, if desired.

# Peanut Butter-Banana Cream Pie

SERVES 12

PER SERVING: 290 CALORIES, 13.5 GRAMS FAT
PER SERVING (SUGAR FREE): 260 CALORIES, 13.5 GRAMS FAT

1 Cream Cheese Pie Crust (page 26) in a 9 × 2-inch pie pan, unbaked, chilled

½ cup fat-free evaporated milk

1 teaspoon unflavored gelatin powder

8 ounces (1 cup) reduced-fat cream cheese (neufchâtel), preferably Kraft brand

½ cup reduced-fat smooth peanut butter, preferably natural style

½ cup sugar

¼ teaspoon salt

¼ cup unsweetened shredded coconut, toasted (optional)

2 ripe large bananas, cut into ¼-inch-thick rounds

2 tablespoons salted roasted peanuts, coarsely chopped

Peanut butter and bananas are a perennial favorite combination, so this pie is always a huge hit. I've made the filling extra creamy by blending whipped fat-free evaporated milk with peanut butter and reduced-fat cream cheese. This is much tastier than simply spreading peanut butter on a banana!

Preheat the oven to 350°F with a rack in the center position.

Prick the bottom of the pie crust all over with a fork and bake it for about 25 minutes, until it is golden brown. Let the crust cool completely, about 30 minutes.

Pour ¼ cup of the evaporated milk into a small saucepan. Whisk in the gelatin and let it stand for 3 minutes to soften. Then cook over medium heat, stirring, until the milk is hot and the gelatin has dissolved completely, about 3 minutes. Do not allow it to boil.

Transfer the hot milk to a small bowl and stir in the remaining ¼ cup of evaporated milk. Freeze for about 10 minutes, or just until the edges of the milk begin to set.

While the milk is chilling, mix the cream cheese and peanut butter with an electric mixer on medium speed for about 1 minute, until well blended. Add the sugar and salt, and beat for 1 minute longer. Set aside.

recipe continues

**MAKE AHEAD!**

The crust can be baked a day ahead and stored at room temperature. The finished pie can be refrigerated, covered, up to 1 day ahead.

**SWEET & SUGAR FREE!**

Substitute 5 tablespoons (18 packets) of Truvía for the sugar in the filling, and omit the sugar in the crust.

Using an electric mixer and clean beaters, beat the chilled milk on high speed for 4 to 5 minutes, until it resembles whipped cream. Add the peanut butter mixture and beat on medium for 1 minute, or until just combined. Stir in half of the toasted coconut, if using.

Spoon about one-third of the peanut butter mixture into the cooled baked crust, smoothing it with a spatula to completely cover the bottom. Distribute the banana slices evenly over the filling. Spread the remaining filling evenly over the bananas. Sprinkle the peanuts evenly over the top, as well as the remaining toasted coconut, if using. Cover the pie with plastic film and refrigerate for at least 1 hour.

*To serve:* Use a sharp knife to cut the pie into 12 wedges.

Refrigerate any leftover pie, tightly covered, for up to 3 days.

# Carrot Cake

## cake

Nonstick pan spray

½ cup raisins, golden or dark

½ cup walnut halves or pieces, toasted

⅔ cup unsweetened shredded coconut, toasted

2 cups very finely shredded carrots (about 2 medium carrots)

2 cups crushed pineapple packed in juice, drained, liquid reserved

2 cups all-purpose flour

½ cup whole wheat flour

1½ cups granulated sugar

2 teaspoons baking soda

1¼ teaspoons ground cinnamon

1 teaspoon salt

¾ cup liquid egg substitute

½ cup plus 2 tablespoons plain nonfat Greek-style yogurt

¼ cup canola oil

## frosting

16 ounces (2 cups) reduced-fat cream cheese (neufchâtel), preferably Kraft brand

1 cup powdered sugar

½ teaspoon finely grated lemon zest

1 teaspoon fresh lemon juice

Carrot cake sounds so innocent—it's made with vegetables, after all. But by the time you add oil, eggs, and nuts and top it with a frosting made with butter and cream cheese, those carrots are transformed into one of the most fattening cakes around. By replacing most of the oil with pineapple juice and nonfat yogurt, using egg substitute, and decreasing the sugar and nuts, the fat and calories are cut by over half, making this cake live up to its virtuous name. Reduced-fat cream cheese provides plenty of richness for the frosting, and lemon juice and zest give it the tangy impression of sour cream.

To make the cake: Preheat the oven to 350°F with a rack in the center position. Coat the bottom and sides of a 10-inch springform or round cake pan with pan spray.

Put the raisins in a bowl and cover with hot tap water. Let stand for 5 minutes to plump, then drain and set aside. Chop the nuts into pea-size pieces. Set aside half of the coconut for the garnish. In a medium bowl, mix together the chopped nuts, drained raisins, carrots, drained pineapple, and the remaining coconut; set aside.

In a large bowl, whisk together the all-purpose and whole wheat flours, sugar, baking soda, cinnamon, and salt. In a small bowl, combine the egg substitute, yogurt, oil, and ⅓ cup of the reserved pineapple juice; whisk until smooth. Whisk the egg mixture into the flour until the batter is thoroughly combined. Fold in the carrot mixture with a rubber spatula until well distributed.

Spread the cake batter evenly in the prepared pan, and bake for 55 to 60 minutes, until a knife inserted into the center comes out with no more than a few crumbs clinging to it. If the top browns before the cake is done, tent a piece of foil lightly over it for the remainder of the baking time.

Let the cake cool in the pan on a wire rack for 30 minutes. Then release the cake from the pan and let it cool directly on the rack for 2 to 3 hours, until completely cool.

To make the frosting: In a medium bowl, using an electric mixer, beat the cream cheese, powdered sugar, lemon zest, and lemon juice on low speed until combined. Increase the speed to medium and beat for another 2 minutes, until the frosting is free of lumps. (If using a standing mixer, use the paddle attachment.)

To finish: Cut the cake in half horizontally to form 2 layers. Place the bottom half cut-side-up on a serving platter, and dollop one-third of the frosting over the cake, then spread it evenly over the cake with an offset spatula. Place the top layer over the frosting, cut-side-down. Use the remaining frosting to cover the sides and then the top in an even layer. Use the spatula or the back of a spoon to make decorative waves and dips on the top of the cake. Press the reserved coconut into the frosting on the sides of the cake with your hands.

To serve: Cut into 16 wedges.

# Banana-Caramel-Chocolate Sundae

SERVES 6

PER SERVING: 385 CALORIES, 9 GRAMS FAT
PER SERVING (SUGAR FREE): 195 CALORIES, 8.5 GRAMS FAT

## ice cream

2 ripe medium bananas

½ cup (packed) dark brown sugar

1 cup 2% milk

1 cup fat-free half-and-half

½ cup liquid egg substitute

¼ cup plain nonfat Greek-style yogurt

½ teaspoon pure vanilla extract

Pinch of salt

1 cup Caramel Sauce (page 32), warmed or at room temperature

3 ripe medium bananas

1 cup Simple Fudge Sauce (page 33), warmed

Luscious Whipped Topping (page 35) or store-bought whipped topping (optional)

Finely chopped toasted almonds (optional)

In one round of the *Food Network Challenge: Ice Cream Clash,* four pastry chefs were asked to make the perfect sundae. Mine took me back to the old-fashioned ice cream parlor in the small town where I grew up, where my favorite sundae overflowed with chocolate, caramel, and bananas. This is a lighter version of my winning entry. The ice cream mixture needn't be cooked because the egg substitute is pasteurized, and the bananas give it extra body. For a party, I like to put out all of the components for everyone to build their own sundae. If you're short on time, make some of the components yourself and purchase the others.

To make the ice cream: Preheat the oven to 350°F with a rack in the center position.

Put the peeled bananas in a baking dish that is just large enough to hold them, and lightly mash them with a fork. Stir in the brown sugar and 2 tablespoons water. Bake for 20 minutes, or until the sugar is bubbling and the bananas are fragrant. Set aside to cool slightly.

Scrape the warm bananas and all of the pan juices into a food processor or blender, and add the milk, half-and-half, egg substitute, yogurt, vanilla, and salt. Blend for about 1 minute, until smooth. Refrigerate the ice cream mixture for several hours, until it is very cold, then freeze it in an ice cream machine according to the manufacturer's directions. Pack it into a container and freeze it overnight, or until scoopable. (If the ice cream is difficult to scoop, allow it to soften for 30 minutes in the refrigerator.)

**SWEET & SUGAR FREE!**

Substitute ¼ cup plus 2¼ tea-spoons (17 packets) of Truvía for the brown sugar in the ice cream. The ice cream will be firmer than one made with sugar, so serve it the day it is made or soften it in the refrigerator or at room temperature before scooping. Use sugar-free toppings, if desired. (See the sugar-free version of the Simple Fudge Sauce on page 33.)

*To serve:* Put the Caramel Sauce into a medium bowl. Cut the bananas into ½-inch-thick rounds and stir them into the caramel.

Spoon 1 tablespoon warm Fudge Sauce into a small (approximately 12-ounce) sundae glass. Top with a ⅓-cup scoop of the ice cream and ⅓ cup of the banana-caramel mixture. Top with another ⅓-cup scoop of ice cream. Finish the sundae with a drizzle of Fudge Sauce (about 1½ teaspoons) and top with whipped topping and almonds, if desired. Repeat to make the remaining sundaes, and serve immediately.

# desserts in a hurry

*Most of us don't have several hours to spare* every time we step into the kitchen. That's why I've dedicated this chapter to recipes that are sweet, skinny, and fast!

Although some recipes in this chapter include optional components that take a little longer, every recipe here can be made, from start to finish, in 30 minutes or less. No long baking times. No waiting for something to chill or set. Just 30 minutes and dessert is on the table.

When you need dessert in a hurry, these recipes will save the day. Staying *Sweet & Skinny* has never been easier.

# Molten Chocolate Soufflé Cake

Nonstick pan spray

½ cup plus 1½ tablespoons semisweet chocolate chips

2 tablespoons (¼ stick) unsalted butter

3 tablespoons unsweetened Dutch-processed cocoa powder

2 tablespoons liquid egg substitute

1½ teaspoons pure vanilla extract

⅛ teaspoon salt

3 egg whites from large eggs, at room temperature

½ teaspoon cream of tartar

⅓ cup sugar

Crème Anglaise (page 34, optional)

MAKE AHEAD!

The unbaked cakes can be refrigerated in the ramekins, covered with plastic film, for up to 5 days, or frozen for up to 2 weeks. If frozen, thaw them overnight in the refrigerator. The cold cakes will take slightly longer to bake—about 8 minutes.

This cake is amazingly rich and chocolatey. With a warm, oozy center, it is the ultimate comfort dessert. Even better, you can prepare it at a moment's notice, and it will impress your guests every time. Chocolate extremists (like me!) prefer this cake on its own, but others might enjoy a spoonful of Crème Anglaise (page 34) over the top.

Preheat the oven to 400°F with a rack in the center position. Coat ten 4-ounce ramekins with pan spray and space them evenly on a rimmed baking sheet.

Combine the chocolate chips, butter, and 2 tablespoons water in a double boiler, or in a bowl in a microwave oven, and heat until you can stir the mixture smooth. Whisk in the cocoa powder, egg substitute, vanilla, and salt. Set aside in a warm spot.

Using a standing mixer fitted with the whisk attachment, beat the egg whites on high speed until they are foamy. Add the cream of tartar, and with the motor running, gradually add the sugar, a few teaspoons at a time. Continue to beat until soft peaks form, curling over softly when you lift the beater. (Alternatively, use a handheld electric mixer.)

Fold the chocolate mixture into the whites just until there are no more visible white streaks.

Spoon the mixture into the prepared ramekins and bake for 5 to 6 minutes, until the tops are slightly puffed, the edges are set, and the center jiggles when you gently shake a ramekin.

To serve: Use oven mitts to carefully transfer the ramekins to serving plates. Serve immediately, with Crème Anglaise spooned over the top, if desired.

# Moscato Sabayon with White Peaches

SERVES 4

PER SERVING: 140 CALORIES, 2.5 GRAMS FAT

2 large eggs

3 tablespoons orange blossom honey or other mild honey

¾ cup moscato (sparkling muscat wine)

2 ripe medium white or yellow peaches, pitted and cut into ¼-inch-thick slices

Sabayon is a magical mixture that is as airy as mousse yet flows like a sauce. It is typically made with egg yolks and sweet wine, but I've used whole eggs for a lighter dessert that is every bit as luscious and satisfying. Moscato is typically fizzy and gently sweet, with a floral aroma and a taste reminiscent of peaches. For this recipe, I like Innocent Bystander, a pink Australian muscat available in half bottles—just enough to enjoy a glass while you whip up this quick dessert.

Put four serving glasses and a large bowl into the refrigerator to chill.

Select a saucepan and a large bowl that will sit over it as a kind of double boiler. Pour about 1 inch of water into the pan—it should not touch the bottom of the bowl when you place the bowl on top. Bring the water to a simmer over medium heat, then reduce the heat to keep it at a slow simmer.

Put the eggs and honey into the bowl and place it atop the saucepan. Use a whisk to vigorously beat the mixture over the simmering water for several minutes, until it is thick and foamy. You will want to keep it constantly moving to avoid scrambling the eggs.

While continuing to whisk, add the wine in a slow, steady stream. Continue to whisk vigorously for about 5 minutes longer, until there is no liquid left in the bottom of the bowl. The mixture will be very thick and about tripled in volume. Remove the bowl from the saucepan and turn off the heat.

Transfer the sabayon to the chilled bowl and beat for 1 minute to cool it slightly.

To serve: Divide the peaches evenly among the chilled serving glasses, and spoon the sabayon over them. Serve immediately.

# Mixed-Berry Dutch Baby

PER SERVING: 150 CALORIES, 2.5 GRAMS FAT

1 tablespoon unsalted butter, melted

½ cup liquid egg substitute

⅓ cup plus 1 tablespoon granulated sugar

1 teaspoon finely grated lemon zest

1 teaspoon pure vanilla extract

⅛ teaspoon salt

⅔ cup 2% milk

⅔ cup all-purpose flour

1½ cups strawberries, hulled and quartered

1 cup raspberries

½ cup blueberries

1 tablespoon powdered sugar

This classic German pancake is a cross between a soufflé and an omelet. The berries are traditionally served on the side, but I have mixed some into the pancake for a dotted effect. As with a soufflé, you'll want to serve this straight from the oven.

Preheat the oven to 450°F with a rack in the center position. Brush a 10-inch cast-iron skillet with the melted butter; set aside.

In a medium bowl, whisk together the egg substitute, sugar, lemon zest, vanilla, and salt. Whisk in the milk. Sift the flour over the mixture and whisk until smooth.

Pour the mixture into the prepared skillet. Top with ⅔ cup of the strawberries and ¼ cup each of the raspberries and blueberries. Combine the remaining berries together in a small bowl.

Bake for 15 minutes, or until the edges are golden brown and the center is cooked through.

To serve: Dust the pancake with powdered sugar, cut into 8 wedges, and serve immediately, dividing the remaining berries among the plates.

# Spiced Chocolate Mousse

PER SERVING: 170 CALORIES, 10 GRAMS FAT

2 tablespoons semisweet chocolate chips

1 cup Cool Whip Lite

1 tablespoon plus 1 teaspoon good-quality unsweetened cocoa powder, natural or Dutch-processed

¼ teaspoon ground cinnamon

Scant ¼ teaspoon cayenne pepper

2 teaspoons pepitas (toasted hulled pumpkin seeds)

½ teaspoon extra virgin olive oil

Pinch of coarse sea salt, such as fleur de sel

Olive oil and sea salt have become an immensely popular pairing with chocolate desserts. Add cayenne and cinnamon to the mix to wake up chocolate's spicy notes, top it with nutty pepitas, and you have a mousse that is rich and flavorful, surprisingly low in fat, and a cinch to make. You can use Luscious Whipped Topping (page 35) in place of the Cool Whip, but it will push you over the 30-minute mark to prepare the dessert.

Combine the chocolate chips and 2 teaspoons water in a double boiler, or in a bowl in a microwave oven, and heat until you can stir the mixture smooth.

Put the whipped topping into a medium bowl and whisk in the melted chocolate until the mixture is smooth. Whisk in the cocoa, cinnamon, and cayenne until they are well combined.

To serve: Divide the mousse between two serving glasses and top with the pepitas. Drizzle the olive oil over the tops, and sprinkle with a small pinch of sea salt.

MAKE AHEAD!

The mousse can be made up to 2 days in advance and refrigerated, tightly covered; add the toppings just before serving.

# Lemon Mousse with Basil and Blueberries

SERVES 2

PER SERVING: 190 CALORIES, 8 GRAMS FAT

3 tablespoons white chocolate chips

⅔ cup Cool Whip Lite or Luscious Whipped Topping (page 35)

½ cup plain nonfat Greek-style yogurt

½ teaspoon finely grated lemon zest, plus more for garnish

½ cup blueberries

2 fresh basil leaves, rolled up and cut crosswise into thin ribbons

**MAKE AHEAD!**

The mousse can be refrigerated, tightly covered, up to 2 days in advance. Layer with the basil and berries just before serving.

This light mousse highlights summer's beautiful berries in a simple yet sophisticated dessert. Yogurt and lemon zest create a tangy dessert with just a hint of lemon. The best part of this mousse: it needs no time to set. For the quickest dessert, use a store-bought topping such as Cool Whip Lite.

Combine the chocolate chips and 2 teaspoons water in a double boiler, or in a bowl in a microwave oven, and heat until you can stir the chocolate smooth.

In a medium bowl, whisk together the whipped topping and yogurt. Whisk in the melted chocolate and the lemon zest.

To serve: Divide half of the mousse evenly between two 6-ounce dessert glasses. Top with half of the berries and half of the basil. Spoon the remaining mousse over each and top with the remaining blueberries, basil, and lemon zest. Serve immediately.

# Rum-Roasted Pineapple with Vanilla Ice Cream

SERVES 6

PER SERVING: 190 CALORIES, 4 GRAMS FAT

Nonstick pan spray

½ ripe small pineapple, peeled and trimmed (not cored)

2 teaspoons unsalted butter

2 tablespoons dark rum

½ cup (packed) dark brown sugar

¼ teaspoon ground ginger

1 vanilla bean

2 cups Vanilla Ice Cream (page 37) or Dreyer's Slow Churned Vanilla Ice Cream

When roasted, slices of pineapple take on a beautifully translucent appearance. Unlike many fruits, pineapple does not sweeten any further after it is picked. To be sure you have a ripe one, look for an overall golden color, with no tinge of green, and a sweet, fragrant aroma near the bottom.

Preheat the oven to 450°F with a rack in the center position. Coat a rimmed baking sheet with pan spray.

Use a thin, sharp knife to cut the pineapple crosswise into twenty-four ⅛-inch-thick slices. Arrange the slices in a single layer on the prepared baking sheet.

Squeeze the pineapple trimmings or some of the remaining pineapple in your fist over a small saucepan, until you have 2 tablespoons juice. Add the butter and 1 tablespoon of the rum and heat for 30 seconds until melted.

In another small bowl, stir together the brown sugar and ginger. Use a paring knife to slit the vanilla bean lengthwise and scrape the seeds into the sugar mixture. Stir the sugar mixture into the pineapple juice–butter mixture to make a sauce. Spoon the sauce over the pineapple slices on the baking sheet.

Bake the pineapple for 15 minutes, or until tender, somewhat translucent, and fragrant. Pour the remaining 1 tablespoon rum over the roasted pineapple, turning the slices to coat them.

To serve: Fan 4 pineapple slices onto each of six individual dessert plates, and spoon the pan sauce over them. Serve the pineapple topped with a ⅓-cup scoop of ice cream.

# Roasted Sesame Bananas

1½ teaspoons unsalted butter

2½ tablespoons fresh orange juice

3 tablespoons (packed) dark brown sugar

¼ teaspoon ground cinnamon

Pinch of salt

1 firm-ripe large banana

⅔ cup Vanilla Ice Cream (page 37) or Dreyer's Slow Churned Vanilla Ice Cream

½ teaspoon toasted sesame seeds

Roasted bananas are an easy and delicious dessert all on their own. In this version, toasted sesame seeds add crunchy contrast and a rich, roasted taste that allows you to cut the butter to a minimum and still create a rich and flavorful dish. Use Browned Butter (page 24) for extra flavor if you have some on hand, but there's no need to make up a batch for this small quantity. Use a banana that is yellow all over, with just a few flecks of brown.

Preheat the oven to 400°F with a rack in the center position. Have on hand a standard loaf pan or other small baking pan.

Melt the butter in a small saucepan over medium heat, or in the microwave. Whisk in the orange juice and 1 teaspoon water. Stir in the brown sugar, cinnamon, and salt until well combined.

Peel the banana, cut it in half crosswise, and then cut each piece in half lengthwise to make 4 pieces. Put the banana pieces into the loaf pan and spoon the sauce over them, turning the pieces in the sauce to coat them completely.

Bake the bananas for 5 minutes. Use a spoon to baste the pieces with the sauce, and then bake for 5 minutes longer.

To serve: Place 2 banana pieces on each plate and top each with a ⅓-cup scoop of ice cream. Spoon the remaining pan sauce over the top, and sprinkle with the sesame seeds.

# Blackberry Napoleon

Nonstick pan spray

¼ cup all-purpose flour

2 tablespoons rolled oats

2 tablespoons (packed) dark brown sugar

½ teaspoon finely grated lemon or orange zest

Pinch of ground cinnamon

Pinch of salt

1 tablespoon unsalted butter

2½ tablespoons light corn syrup or brown rice syrup

¾ cup Quick Sour Cream Whipped Topping (page 36)

2½ cups blackberries

In the restaurants I have worked in, we've always kept a quick cookie dough on hand for making what we call snap cookies. Used for garnishes and simple desserts, the buttery cookie holds up well and keeps its crunchy texture. A snap cookie made with oats and brown sugar complements the berries and sour cream in this quick napoleon. The broken cookie shards give the dessert a contemporary look. They won't weigh down the berries, or you!

Preheat the oven to 350°F with a rack in the center position. Line a baking sheet with a silicone baking mat or parchment paper. Coat the mat or paper with pan spray.

In a small bowl, whisk together the flour, oats, brown sugar, lemon zest, cinnamon, and salt; set aside.

Melt the butter in a small saucepan over medium heat. Whisk in the corn syrup and 1 tablespoon water. Add this to the flour mixture, stirring vigorously to form a spreadable batter.

Use an offset spatula to spread the batter as thin as possible on the prepared baking sheet. It should cover most of the sheet. Bake for 15 minutes, or until the cookie is golden brown.

Remove the baking sheet from the oven and immediately slide the baking mat off the sheet. Let the cookie rest on the sheet for about 2 minutes to cool and harden. Then break it with your hands into 18 roughly equal-size pieces.

To serve: Lay a cookie on an individual dessert plate and top with 1 tablespoon of the whipped topping and 3 or 4 berries. Repeat with a second layer, then top with a third cookie. Repeat to form the remaining napoleons. Serve immediately.

# Dessert Pizza with Cherries and Rosemary

Nonstick pan spray (if using parchment paper)

1 package (about 14 ounces) fresh or frozen pizza dough (thawed if frozen)

½ cup pitted fresh Bing cherries

Four 4-inch sprigs fresh rosemary

1 tablespoon extra virgin olive oil

2 tablespoons sugar

⅛ teaspoon ground cinnamon

½ cup crumbled Gorgonzola cheese

This pizza is a great choice for those times when you can't decide whether to go sweet or savory. It offers a bit of everything: herbal rosemary, sweet Bing cherries, and tangy-salty Gorgonzola cheese. Use a good-quality dough—one with no additives or preservatives. A glass of port is a perfect companion.

Preheat the oven to 500°F with a rack in the upper third of the oven. Line a baking sheet with a silicone baking mat, or with parchment paper sprayed with pan spray.

Use your hands to stretch the dough into a 10-inch round of even thickness. Lay the dough on the prepared baking sheet.

Dot the dough evenly with the cherries, and press a rosemary sprig lightly onto each quarter. Brush the dough—including the cherries and rosemary—with the olive oil. Stir the sugar and cinnamon together and sprinkle this evenly over the top.

Bake the pizza for 10 to 12 minutes, until the edges are golden brown. Let cool for 5 minutes.

To serve: Cut the pizza into 8 wedges, transfer the slices to individual plates, and sprinkle the Gorgonzola over the top.

Once it is completely cool, refrigerate any leftover pizza, wrapped in foil, for up to 2 days. Crisp in a hot oven or toaster oven to serve.

# Mocha Affogato Milkshake

PER SERVING: 190 CALORIES, 7 GRAMS FAT

2 cups reduced-fat chocolate brownie ice cream, such as Ben & Jerry's

½ cup nonfat vanilla yogurt

½ cup brewed coffee, at room temperature

¼ cup Kahlúa

1 teaspoon instant espresso powder

1⅓ cups crushed ice

¼ cup Luscious Whipped Topping (page 35) or store-bought topping

1 teaspoon good-quality unsweetened cocoa powder, natural or Dutch-processed

This Italian dessert is made by pouring hot espresso over ice cream (*affogato* means "drowned"). I've turned the idea into a frosty milkshake made with ice cream, coffee, and Kahlúa. Chocolate brownie ice cream provides texture, with little brownie bites speckling this thick and creamy indulgence. (See photo on page 128.)

Put four tall glasses in the freezer to chill.

Blend the ice cream, yogurt, coffee, Kahlúa, espresso powder, and ice in a blender for 30 seconds, until the mixture is thick and creamy, with bite-size brownie chunks.

To serve: Pour the mixture into the chilled glasses. Top with the whipped topping, and sift the cocoa over the shakes.

# Peach Sundaes with Muscat Syrup

## syrup

¾ cup sugar

½ vanilla bean

One 4 × 1-inch strip lemon zest

⅔ cup sweet muscat wine

2 ripe medium yellow peaches, pitted and cut into ½-inch-thick slices

1 pint (2 cups) Peach Sorbet (page 132)

8 amaretto cookies

MAKE AHEAD!

The syrup can be made up to 1 month in advance and refrigerated in a tightly covered container (leave the lemon zest and vanilla bean in the syrup if you wish to deepen its flavor). Bring the syrup to a simmer before pouring it over the peaches.

With just a few ingredients, you can make this sophisticated dessert in no time. Use the small, crunchy amaretto cookies for the best contrast with the smooth sorbet. Nectarines or apricots also work well in this recipe. If you're feeling ambitious (and have more than 30 minutes), forgo store-bought and try making your own Peach Sorbet (page 132). You won't need all of the syrup—save the rest to drizzle over ice cream or fruit, or to mix into drinks.

To make the syrup: In a small saucepan, combine the sugar, vanilla bean, lemon zest, and ½ cup water; stir over medium-high heat. When the mixture boils and all of the sugar has dissolved, stir in the wine and cook for 1 minute. Remove from the heat.

Put the peach slices into a small bowl and pour ½ cup of the hot syrup over them, retaining the lemon zest and vanilla bean in the syrup.

To serve: Scoop the sorbet into four dessert bowls, top with the peaches and syrup, and crush the amaretto cookies over the sundaes. Serve immediately.

# Gingersnap Apple Pie Parfaits

SERVES 6

PER SERVING: 230 CALORIES, 5 GRAMS FAT

12 gingersnap cookies, such as Nabisco Ginger Snaps

¼ cup plus 1 tablespoon sugar

3 large firm apples, such as Fuji, peeled, cored, and diced into ½-inch pieces

½ teaspoon ground cinnamon

⅛ cup brandy

2 teaspoons fresh lemon juice

3 cups Vanilla Ice Cream (page 37) or Dreyer's Slow Churned Vanilla Ice Cream

**When I'm craving apple pie but am pressed for time, this parfait is the perfect solution. It's ready in a snap, and it tastes just like the apple pie my grandmother used to labor over for hours.**

Put the gingersnaps in a plastic bag, seal it, and use a meat tenderizer, hammer, or rolling pin to crush the cookies into large crumbs.

In a large skillet, stir the sugar with ⅓ cup plus 1 tablespoon water over medium-high heat until the water begins to bubble. Add the apples and cinnamon, stirring to evenly coat and cook the apples. Cook for 5 minutes, or until the apples are tender but still a little bit crisp.

Add the brandy and flame it, either by carefully tilting the pan away from you if you are using a gas stove, or by carefully lighting it with a long match or lighter. Remember to wear your oven mitts. Cook for 1 minute to burn off the alcohol. Stir in the lemon juice.

To serve: Spoon half of the hot apples into six parfait or sundae glasses, using about ¼ cup for each. Top each with a ¼-cup scoop of ice cream and sprinkle with a generous tablespoon of crushed gingersnaps, using about half of the crushed cookies. Add another ¼-cup scoop of ice cream to each parfait, and divide the remaining apples over the ice cream. Sprinkle the remaining crushed cookies over the parfaits and serve immediately.

# No-Bake Cheesecake Cups with Concord Grapes

SERVES 4

PER SERVING: 240 CALORIES, 12 GRAMS FAT

6 ounces (¾ cup) Kraft reduced-fat cream cheese (neufchâtel)

¼ cup powdered sugar

⅔ cup frozen whipped topping, such as Cool Whip Lite

1 cup Concord grapes, halved, seeds removed

⅓ cup finely ground honey graham cracker crumbs

Anyone who has enjoyed the combination of grape jelly and cream cheese could guess that Concord grapes would be a great match for cheesecake. Lightened with whipped topping, the cheesecake takes on the silky texture of a mousse. Fresh Concord grapes give these cups a vibrant burst of flavor and juice. The frozen whipped topping helps the cheesecake mixture to chill and set quickly. If you use a thawed whipped topping, the cheesecakes will need about 2 hours in the refrigerator to set.

MAKE AHEAD!

Refrigerate the half-filled glasses and the bowl of remaining cheesecake mixture, tightly covered, for up to 3 days. Assemble with the graham cracker crumbs, grapes, and remaining cheesecake mixture immediately before serving.

Using a standing mixer fitted with the paddle attachment, mix the cream cheese and powdered sugar on medium speed for 30 seconds, just until combined. Add the frozen whipped topping and beat for 1 minute longer, until the mixture is smooth and free of lumps.

Spoon about ¼ cup of the cheesecake mixture into four clear-glass ramekins or serving glasses. Freeze for 25 minutes to firm the cheesecakes. Place the bowl with the remaining cheesecake mixture in the freezer as well.

To serve: Divide the grapes among the chilled cheesecakes, holding back 8 grape halves for garnish. Divide all of the graham cracker crumbs among the cups, sprinkling it over the tops. Spoon the remaining cheesecake mixture from the bowl over the cups, dividing it evenly among them. Top each cup with 2 grape halves, and serve immediately.

# Plum and Rosewater Soup

5 large red plums, pitted and roughly chopped (about 2⅓ cups)

½ cup light agave nectar

2 to 4 tablespoons sugar (depending on the ripeness of the plums)

2 teaspoons fresh lemon juice

2½ teaspoons rosewater

2 strawberries, hulled and cut into paper-thin slices

Vanilla Ice Cream (page 37) or Dreyer's Slow Churned Vanilla Ice Cream (optional)

Rosewater's delicately floral flavor is the perfect accompaniment for summer's ripe plums, creating a dessert that is easy to prepare and unforgettable to taste. Use the most flavorful, perfectly ripe plums you can find, and include the peels—you will be amazed at how much flavor they contribute to this soup.

Place four dessert bowls in the freezer.

Process the plums and agave nectar in a blender or food processor until the mixture is smooth.

Transfer the mixture to a small saucepan and stir in 2 tablespoons of the sugar. Taste, and add up to 2 tablespoons more sugar if needed. Cook the soup over medium heat, stirring occasionally, for about 5 minutes, or until it is bubbling gently. Strain the soup through a fine-mesh strainer into a medium bowl, pushing on the solids with a spoon to extract as much of the juices and flavor as possible. Discard the solids.

Stir in the lemon juice. Set the bowl over a larger bowl of ice water, then carefully place the bowls in the freezer. Freeze for 20 minutes, whisking every 5 minutes or so, until the soup is thoroughly chilled. Remove the bowl from the freezer and stir in the rosewater.

To serve: Ladle the cold soup into the chilled bowls, float the strawberry slices on top, and add a small scoop of ice cream, if using.

# Cinnamon-Sugar Angel Food Cake with Cherries Jubilee

SERVES 4

PER SERVING: 260 CALORIES, 0 GRAMS FAT

¼ cup sugar

¼ teaspoon ground cinnamon

⅓ unglazed Rosemary Angel Food Cake (page 155; made with or without rosemary) or one-third of a 10-inch store-bought angel food cake, cut into 24 1-inch cubes

2 teaspoons cornstarch

¼ cup fresh orange juice

1 cup Bing cherries, fresh or frozen, pitted

¼ teaspoon pure almond extract

1 tablespoon plus 1 teaspoon brandy

½ teaspoon fresh lemon juice

Squares of angel food cake are coated with cinnamon-sugar and toasted just long enough to give the edges a delicate crunch. The addition of warm, juicy cherries makes this a light and playful dessert.

Preheat the broiler on low, with a rack in the center position. Line a rimmed baking sheet with a silicone baking mat or parchment paper.

In a small bowl, stir 1½ tablespoons of the sugar with the cinnamon. Dip the cake cubes into the cinnamon-sugar to coat them on all sides, placing them on the prepared baking sheet as you finish them.

In a small saucepan, stir the cornstarch with the remaining 2½ table-spoons sugar. Stir in 2 tablespoons water to make a smooth paste, then stir in the orange juice. Cook over medium heat, whisking constantly, for 2 minutes, or until the mixture begins to thicken. Add the cherries and cook for 5 minutes longer, until they are tender. Add the almond extract and the brandy.

Using oven mitts, carefully tip the pan away from you to light the sauce with the flame of your gas stove, then set it back over the heat, until the flame dies down. (Alternatively, cook it an extra minute or two to evaporate the alcohol.) Stir in the lemon juice; set aside.

Place the sheet of cake cubes under the broiler and toast them for 3 minutes, or until the edges begin to brown and crisp. Remove the baking sheet from the oven, carefully turn the cake pieces over, and return to the broiler for 1 minute longer.

To serve: Place 6 toasted cake cubes on each plate, and top with the cherries and sauce.

# Port-Roasted Figs with Yogurt and Thyme

SERVES 6

PER SERVING: 320 CALORIES, 2 GRAMS FAT

⅓ cup plus 1 tablespoon sugar

¼ cup tawny port

2 tablespoons honey

Twelve 2-inch sprigs fresh thyme

24 ripe Mission or other black figs, stemmed

3 cups plain nonfat Greek-style yogurt

3 tablespoons sliced almonds, toasted

In restaurants where I've worked, I've kept a version of this fig and yogurt parfait up my sleeve for those times when a patron requested a fruit plate as an alternative to the decadent desserts on the menu. They were always elated to see this come to the table instead of apple slices fanned out on a plate. This is a quick and easy variation of that delightful dessert.

Preheat the oven to 350°F with a rack in the center position.

In a small saucepan, stir together the sugar, port, honey, and ¼ cup water. Set aside the 6 prettiest thyme sprigs for garnish, and drop the other 6 into the pan. Bring the mixture to a boil over medium heat, then boil for 2 minutes, or until the sugar dissolves and the syrup thickens slightly.

Cut the figs in half from top to bottom and place them in a 9 × 13-inch baking dish. Pour the hot syrup over the figs and bake for 10 minutes, until the figs are warm and softened. Pick out and discard the thyme sprigs.

To serve: Spoon half of the warm figs, along with some of the pan sauce, into six parfait glasses. Spoon ½ cup of the yogurt over each; then top with the remaining figs and sauce. Sprinkle with the toasted almonds, and garnish each glass with one of the reserved thyme sprigs.

# Midnight Breakfast

Coffee-Bourbon Caramel Sauce
(page 32)

3 ripe (but not brown) large
bananas, peeled and cut into
½-inch-thick rounds

1 quart Vanilla Ice Cream
(page 37) or Dreyer's Slow
Churned Vanilla Ice Cream

½ cup slightly crushed Cap'n
Crunch cereal

A late-night sweets craving can be difficult to resist, especially if you have co-conspirators to urge you on. This is the perfect solution—half breakfast, half dessert, and a hit of bourbon to send you sweetly off to sleep.

Prepare the caramel sauce and let it cool for 15 to 20 minutes, until it is warm. Add the bananas, stirring gently to coat them.

*To serve:* Divide half of the fruit and sauce among eight parfait glasses. Scoop the vanilla ice cream over the bananas. Spoon the remaining bananas and caramel sauce over the ice cream, and sprinkle the crushed cereal over the top.

*desserts in a hurry* 111

# Palm Sundaes

PER SERVING: 370 CALORIES, 4 GRAMS FAT

10 large Medjool dates

½ cup fresh orange juice

¼ cup dark rum

3 tablespoons honey

6 green cardamom pods

One 3-inch cinnamon stick

2 cups coconut sorbet

¼ cup crushed chocolate wafer cookies or chocolate graham crackers

I was first served the combination of dates, coconut sorbet, and chocolate wafers in my own kitchen, by a friend who was astounded that I had nothing planned for dessert. Facing a room full of disapproving looks, I jumped up to rummage through the pantry, when my friend took over. He reached for some dates I had purchased at the farmers' market, unearthed coconut sorbet in my freezer, and grabbed a bag of chocolate cookies. It was a fantastic combination! In this variation of what has become a staple in my dessert repertoire, I've dressed up the dates with a spiced rum sauce. Like the original, it is a beautiful last-minute dessert that is much more than the sum of its humble parts. It is also a fitting tribute to the palm tree, which gives us both dates and coconuts.

MAKE AHEAD!

The rum sauce can be made up to 4 days ahead and refrigerated, tightly covered, before composing the sundaes.

Bring a medium saucepan of water to a boil.

Cut a small "X" in the bottom of each date. Drop the dates into the boiling water and blanch for 1 to 2 minutes, until the skin begins to peel away from the flesh at the "X". Drain the dates in a colander and run them under cool water for 30 seconds, until they are cool enough to touch. Pull the skin from the dates, cut them in half lengthwise, and remove the pits.

In a small saucepan, bring the orange juice, rum, honey, cardamom pods, and cinnamon stick to a simmer over medium heat. Add the dates and cook for 5 minutes, until the sauce thickens slightly. Remove the cardamom and cinnamon.

To serve: Scoop the coconut sorbet into four bowls. Distribute the dates over the sorbet, spooning the rum sauce over the top. Sprinkle with the crushed chocolate cookies.

# sweet treats

## For me, dessert is not just for special occasions!

I have never found depriving myself of sweets to be a productive way of staying on the *Sweet & Skinny* path. In fact, hardly a day goes by when I don't indulge in some sweet morsel—a bite-size cookie, a few spoonfuls of frozen yogurt. It doesn't have to be much, just enough to keep my sweet tooth satisfied.

This chapter is all about those kinds of quick and simple snacks. Most of these treats keep well for at least a week. This is ideal because, let's face it, they wouldn't be as rewarding if you had to whip up a new batch every day. Whether you are looking for a cup of hot chocolate at the end of the day or a cool and refreshing popsicle on a summer afternoon, this chapter is loaded with fast and easy treats to get you sweetly through the day.

# Vanilla, Coconut, and Peppermint Marshmallows

### MAKES 30 MARSHMALLOWS
#### PER MARSHMALLOW: 40 CALORIES, 0 GRAMS FAT

## vanilla marshmallows

2 tablespoons powdered sugar

¼ cup egg whites (from about 2 small eggs)

1 tablespoon plus 2 teaspoons unflavored gelatin powder

1⅓ cups granulated sugar

1 teaspoon pure vanilla extract

Nonstick pan spray, for coating the spatula

MAKE AHEAD!

The marshmallows can remain in the pan at room temperature, tightly covered, for up to 1 week. Remove just what you will use, leaving any remaining marshmallows in the pan and covering the pan tightly with plastic film.

Marshmallows are such a nostalgic sweet treat for me—I still insist on toasting some over the fire when I go camping. The first time I made my own, I felt anything but nostalgic. The recipe for those sweet pillows was intimidating! Well, I have found a way to make them easy enough to tackle at home.

Sift 1 tablespoon of the powdered sugar over the bottom of a 9-inch square pan. Put the egg whites into a large bowl. Put the gelatin into a small bowl and stir in 5 tablespoons water, continuing to stir until it is completely softened, about 1 minute. Set these all aside.

In a small nonreactive saucepan (stainless steel or copper works best; avoid nonstick), stir the granulated sugar with ⅓ cup water to completely moisten the sugar. Bring the mixture to a boil over medium heat, using a pastry brush dipped into cold water to brush any sugar crystals from the sides of the pan.

Cook the sugar without stirring until it measures 240°F on a candy thermometer, then remove the saucepan from the heat. (Alternatively, have ready a small bowl of ice water. The sugar is ready when ½ teaspoon of the hot syrup dropped into the ice water forms a soft ball that you can roll between your fingers. Avoid cooking longer than this stage.)

Use your fingers to break up and drop the dissolved gelatin into the sugar syrup. Let stand for 30 seconds, then stir to completely dissolve the gelatin.

Using a standing mixer fitted with the whisk attachment, beat the egg whites on high speed until they are foamy. (Alternatively, use a hand-held electric mixer.) With the mixer running, add the syrup in a slow, steady stream, pouring it between the edge of the bowl and the whisk to avoid splattering. After all of the syrup is in, continue beating the whites for 4 to 5 minutes, until the bottom of the bowl is no longer hot to the touch. Add the vanilla and beat for 1 minute longer.

Coat a heatproof spatula with pan spray to prevent sticking, and use the spatula to quickly spread the mixture smoothly and evenly into the prepared pan. Sift the remaining 1 tablespoon powdered sugar over the marshmallow. Wrap the pan tightly with plastic film and set it aside at room temperature for at least 1 hour.

To serve: Cut the marshmallow into 6 strips in one direction, then 5 strips in the other direction, to make 30 marshmallows.

Coconut Marshmallows Substitute ½ teaspoon pure coconut extract for the vanilla extract. Instead of sifting the second tablespoon of powdered sugar over the top at the end, sprinkle with ¼ cup toasted unsweetened shredded coconut.

Peppermint Marshmallows Substitute ½ teaspoon pure peppermint extract for the vanilla extract. Instead of sifting the second tablespoon of powdered sugar over the top at the end, sprinkle with ¼ cup crushed peppermint candies.

# Strawberry-Black Pepper Macarons

MAKES 28 MACARONS

PER MACARON: 60 CALORIES, 1.5 GRAMS FAT

⅔ cup slivered blanched almonds

1¼ cups powdered sugar

1 teaspoon freshly ground black
   pepper (ground as fine as
   possible)

3 egg whites from large eggs

¼ teaspoon cream of tartar

¼ cup granulated sugar

¼ teaspoon liquid red food
   coloring

½ cup strawberry jam

## MAKING PERFECT MACARONS

The way the macarons lie on the baking sheet after you pipe them is a clue to how well the batter was mixed. If they stand up in a point like a chocolate kiss, the batter was undermixed. If this happens, scrape the mixture back into the bowl and fold it a little longer to break down the meringue. If the mixture spreads or runs significantly after piping, you may have overmixed the batter—go ahead and bake the macarons anyway. If the tops gently flatten on their own, they were mixed just right and your cookies should be perfect!

Macarons are among the most beautiful and elegant cookies. The petite French sandwich cookie is made light with egg whites, but the fillings are typically rich with butter and cream. In these macarons, I fill the delicate cookies with jam for lots of flavor without the fat. Proper mixing technique is the key to light macarons. With these instructions, you will feel like a true French *pâtissier*.

Line two rimmed baking sheets with silicone baking mats or parchment paper.

Process the almonds and powdered sugar in a food processor for 1 minute, or until the nuts are very fine. Scrape the mixture into a medium-mesh strainer placed over a medium bowl, and strain, discarding any pieces that are too large to fit through the holes. Stir in the black pepper; set aside.

Using a standing mixer fitted with the whisk attachment, beat the egg whites on high speed until they are foamy. (Alternatively, use a handheld electric mixer.) Add the cream of tartar and mix until it is incorporated. With the mixer running, gradually add the sugar, a few teaspoons at a time. Continue to mix just until medium peaks form, no longer. They should curl over softly when you lift the beater. Add the food coloring, mixing just until the whites are evenly colored.

Fold half of the almond mixture into the whites with several quick, sweeping strokes. Once it is mostly incorporated, fold in the remaining almond mixture, mixing just until the mixture is combined. The batter should be smooth and glossy, but not so loose that it will run when piped.

recipe continues

Overmixed batter *(left)*,
perfectly mixed batter *(center)*,
and undermixed batter *(right)*.

Spoon the mixture into a piping bag fitted with a #4 round tip. (Alternatively, use a resealable plastic bag: fill, press out the air, seal, and snip off one corner.) Pipe fifty-six 1½-inch rounds of the batter onto the prepared baking sheets, spacing them about ¾ inch apart.

Lift and tap the baking sheets firmly against a flat surface several times to release any air bubbles. Set the sheets aside at room temperature for 30 minutes.

While the macarons are resting, preheat the oven to 320°F with racks in the upper and lower thirds of the oven.

Bake the macarons for 10 to 12 minutes. Rotate the baking sheets from top to bottom and front to back, and bake for 5 minutes longer. Place the sheets on wire racks and let them cool for at least 20 minutes, or until you can easily peel the meringues from the baking mats or parchment.

Spoon ¾ teaspoon of jam onto the bottom of one cookie and gently press the bottom of a second cookie over the jam to make a sandwich. Repeat with the remaining cookies and jam.

Store the cookies at room temperature in an airtight container, separating the layers with waxed paper, for up to 5 days.

Chocolate-Raspberry Macarons Substitute 1 teaspoon unsweetened cocoa powder (natural or Dutch-processed) for the black pepper, and omit the food coloring. For the filling, melt ⅓ cup semisweet chocolate chips with 1 tablespoon water in a double boiler until you can stir it smooth. (Alternatively, use a microwave oven.) Whisk in ⅓ cup raspberry jam.

# Kourabiethes

Nonstick pan spray

¼ cup Browned Butter (page 24), softened

1 tablespoon plus 1 teaspoon reduced-fat cream cheese (neufchâtel)

2 teaspoons non-hydrogenated shortening, such as Spectrum brand

2 tablespoons plus 1 teaspoon powdered sugar, plus about ⅓ cup more for finishing

1 tablespoon liquid egg substitute

2 teaspoons Metaxa or brandy

1 tablespoon pure vanilla extract

¾ to 1 cup all-purpose flour

⅛ teaspoon salt

*Kourabiethes* (koo-rah-byeh-thes) are traditional Greek butter cookies, similar to Mexican wedding cookies. The first Greek cookie I learned to make, these are based on my grandmother Vasiliki's recipe. When she was a young woman, the king of Greece came to visit her town of Megalopolis. My grandmother spent days kneading her batch by hand. When the king sampled the cookies, he declared hers the best he had ever tasted. It wasn't easy creating a light version that could hold court with the original, but these pleased even my grandmother. The trick is using Browned Butter (page 24), a little shortening, and plenty of mixing time.

Preheat the oven to 350°F with a rack in the center position. Coat a baking sheet with pan spray.

Using a standing mixer fitted with the paddle attachment, beat the butter, cream cheese, shortening, and 2 tablespoons plus 1 teaspoon powdered sugar on medium speed for 10 minutes. (Alternatively, use a handheld electric mixer.) Add the egg substitute, Metaxa, and vanilla, and beat for 2 minutes longer. Add ¾ cup flour and the salt; mix for 10 minutes more. If the dough is sticky, continue to add flour, 1 tablespoon at a time, until it is smooth and no longer sticky.

Transfer the dough to a lightly floured surface and pat it into a ½-inch-thick disk. Cut out the cookies with a 1½-inch cutter, gently gathering and repatting the scraps as needed to make about 20 cookies. (To form the cookies without a cutter, divide the dough into 4 equal pieces. Roll 1 piece back and forth under your palms on a flat surface to make a 1-inch-diameter log. Press down on the log with your palms to form a

recipe continues

long, flat strip, ½ inch thick. Cut the strip crosswise into 5 pieces. Repeat with the remaining 3 pieces of dough.)

Transfer the cookies to the prepared baking sheet, placing them ½ inch apart (they will not spread). Bake for 25 to 30 minutes, until the bottoms are golden. Transfer the cookies directly to a wire rack to cool.

Put ⅓ cup powdered sugar in a wide, shallow bowl and drop in several cookies, rolling them in the sugar to evenly coat them. Transfer to a plate. Repeat to coat all of the cookies, adding more sugar if needed. Sift any sugar remaining in the bowl over the tops of the cookies.

Store any leftover cookies in an airtight container at room temperature for up to 2 weeks.

# Papaya-Mint Popsicles

SERVES 6

PER SERVING: 90 CALORIES, 0 GRAMS FAT

1 Hawaiian papaya

⅓ cup fresh orange juice

¼ cup fresh lime juice

¼ cup plus 1 tablespoon agave nectar

2 tablespoons chopped fresh mint

I always looked forward to the times when my mother would make papaya with fresh mint and lime as a breakfast treat. These sophisticated, refreshing popsicles are a frozen tribute to those special mornings. (See photo on page 124.)

Use a vegetable peeler to remove the skin from the papaya. Cut the fruit in half, then spoon out and discard the seeds. Roughly chop the flesh.

Blend the papaya with the orange juice, lime juice, and agave nectar in a blender or food processor for several minutes, until the mixture is smooth. Add the mint and pulse several times to combine, until it is in small flecks.

Pour the mixture into six popsicle molds, snap on the tops, and freeze for at least 6 hours.

*To serve:* Pull each popsicle from the mold with the handle attached. If the popsicle is stubborn, briefly submerge the mold in warm water and try again.

MAKE AHEAD!

The popsicles can remain in their molds in the freezer for up to 1 week.

NO POPSICLE MOLDS?

Try using small plastic containers such as yogurt or pudding cups. Cut a slit through each lid just big enough to fit a popsicle stick. Pour the popsicle mixture into the containers, cover with the lids, and freeze until the mixture is slushy enough to hold the stick upright. Push the sticks through the slits in the lids and continue to freeze until the popsicles are frozen solid.

# Strawberry-Watermelon Popsicles

SERVES 8

PER SERVING: 70 CALORIES, 0 GRAMS FAT

2 cups strawberries, hulled

2 cups cubed watermelon

⅓ cup plus 1 tablespoon agave nectar

At the peak of summer, when strawberries are fragrant and watermelon is sweet, these popsicles make a refreshing treat. They are simple to make and only require that you use fruit that is sweet and flavorful. If you don't have popsicle molds, see page 123 for a quick trick.

MAKE AHEAD!

The popsicles can remain in their molds in the freezer for up to 1 week.

Blend the strawberries, watermelon, and agave nectar in a blender or food processor until the mixture is completely smooth.

Pour the mixture into eight popsicle molds, snap on the tops, and freeze until the popsicles are frozen solid, about 6 hours.

To serve: Pull each popsicle from the mold with the handle attached. If the popsicle is stubborn, briefly submerge the mold in warm water and then try again.

Strawberry-Watermelon Popsicles and Papaya-Mint Popsicles (page 123).

# Piña Colada Popsicles

PER SERVING: 120 CALORIES, 1 GRAM FAT

One 8-ounce can crushed pineapple packed in juice, drained

⅔ cup light coconut milk

½ cup agave nectar

1 teaspoon coconut extract, imitation or natural

Finely grated zest of ½ lime

Juice of ½ lime

Pinch of fine sea salt

MAKE AHEAD!

The popsicles can remain in their molds in the freezer for up to 1 week.

These popsicles taste just like a piña colada, but without the rum. Leave the mixture a little chunky to enjoy some texture in the pops. McCormick's imitation coconut extract delivers the classic flavor of Malibu rum; you can use a natural coconut extract for a more authentic coconut flavor. If you don't have popsicle molds, see page 123 for a quick trick.

Combine the pineapple, coconut milk, agave nectar, coconut extract, lime zest and juice, and salt in a blender or food processor. Pulse until well combined but not completely smooth.

Pour the mixture into six popsicle molds, snap on the tops, and freeze until the popsicles are frozen solid, about 6 hours.

To serve: Pull each popsicle from the mold with the handle attached. If the popsicle is stubborn, briefly submerge the mold in warm water and try again.

# Cucumber-Sake Granita

PER SERVING: 60 CALORIES, 0 GRAMS FAT

1½ cups chopped peeled, seeded English cucumber

1½ cups cubed honeydew melon

¼ cup purified or bottled water

¼ cup sake

3½ tablespoons agave nectar

1 tablespoon fresh lemon juice

2 tablespoons chopped fresh mint, plus additional leaves for garnish

I discovered the classic Japanese combination of cucumber and sake while working in restaurants serving Asian-influenced cuisine. Combined with sweet honeydew melon, these flavors make a refreshing and memorable granita, perfect for creating a sophisticated snow cone during the hot months of summer.

Blend the cucumber, melon, and water in a blender or food processor to break up the flesh. Add the sake, agave nectar, and lemon juice and continue to blend until almost smooth. Add the mint and pulse several times, until the mint is in small flecks.

Transfer the mixture to a 9 × 13-inch pan. Freeze for 30 minutes, or until it is slushy. Stir and scrape the mixture with a fork to break up the ice crystals, then continue to freeze, stirring every 20 minutes, for another 60 to 80 minutes, until the mixture is frozen into icy flakes.

To serve: Scoop the granita into six bowls, and garnish with mint leaves.

Freeze any leftover granita, covered tightly with plastic film, for up to 1 week; fluff it with a fork before serving.

Star Anise Horchata (*left*)
and Mocha Affogato Milkshake
(*right*, see page 101 for recipe).

# Star Anise Horchata

PER SERVING: 90 CALORIES, 0 GRAMS FAT
PER SERVING (SUGAR FREE): 45 CALORIES, 0 GRAMS FAT

1 cup nonfat milk

Three 3-inch cinnamon sticks

1 star anise pod

One 2 × ½-inch strip of orange zest

¼ cup sugar

2 tablespoons rice flour

Finely grated orange zest, for garnish

**SWEET & SUGAR FREE!**

Substitute 1 to 1¾ tablespoons (4 to 5 packets) of Truvía, according to taste, for the sugar.

*Horchata* is a traditional Mexican summertime refresher made with ground rice, milk, and cinnamon. Star anise adds a subtle licorice flavor to this version. Available in the international aisle of most supermarkets, rice flour is more convenient than grinding the rice. This also makes a refreshing alcohol-free summer cocktail.

Heat the milk in a small saucepan over medium heat for 10 minutes, until it is reduced by about one-third. Add the cinnamon sticks, star anise, orange zest, and 2 cups water; cook for 10 minutes longer.

In a medium bowl, stir together the sugar and rice flour. Stir in the hot milk to dissolve the sugar and flour. Refrigerate, loosely covered with plastic film, for 3 to 4 hours, until the horchata is cold.

To serve: Strain the horchata into a pitcher and stir again just before pouring. Pour into four ice-filled glasses and garnish with orange zest.

# "Almond Joy" Macaroons

MAKES APPROXIMATELY 30 MACAROONS

PER MACAROON: 90 CALORIES, 4.5 GRAMS FAT

PER MACAROON (SUGAR FREE): 60 CALORIES, 4.5 GRAMS FAT

⅓ cup crushed pineapple packed in juice, drained

1¾ cups unsweetened shredded coconut

1 cup sugar

¾ cup egg whites (from about 5 large eggs), or ¾ cup liquid egg whites

¼ cup all-purpose flour

⅛ teaspoon salt

½ teaspoon pure vanilla extract

Nonstick pan spray (if not using a baking mat)

About 30 whole almonds, skin on

¼ cup semisweet chocolate chips

SWEET & SUGAR FREE!

Substitute 6 tablespoons plus 2½ teaspoons (26 packets) of Truvía for the sugar. Omit the flour and increase the pineapple to ⅔ cup. If the dough is too dry to scoop, stir in 1 tablespoon water before scooping. Bake the cookies for 15 to 20 minutes.

As a child, I loved coconut desserts: macaroons, coconut cake, and especially the chocolate-and-coconut Almond Joy candy bar. I haven't eaten one of those in many years, but I do eat these cookies, designed to be reminiscent of the candy but not so cloyingly sweet. In this version, pineapple replaces some of the coconut for natural sweetness with fewer calories.

Put the pineapple, coconut, sugar, egg whites, flour, and salt into a medium saucepan and cook over medium-high heat, stirring constantly, for 5 to 6 minutes, until all of the liquid has evaporated and the mixture is sticky. Remove from the heat, stir in the vanilla, and refrigerate for at least 1 hour or up to 2 weeks.

To bake the cookies, preheat the oven to 350°F with a rack in the center position. Coat a baking sheet with pan spray or line it with a silicone baking mat.

Scoop out tablespoon-size balls of the mixture to make about 30 cookies. Arrange the cookies on the prepared baking sheet, spacing them about ½ inch apart (they will not spread). Press an almond into the top of each cookie. Bake for 20 to 25 minutes, until the cookies are golden brown. Halfway through the baking time, rotate the pan from front to back. Transfer the cookies to a wire rack and let them cool completely, about 1 hour.

Melt the chocolate in the top of a double boiler until you can stir it smooth. (Alternatively, use a microwave oven.) Spoon the melted chocolate over the cookies in a zigzag pattern. Allow the chocolate to harden before serving.

Store the cookies in an airtight container at room temperature for up to 1 week.

# Peach Sorbet

1⅓ pounds (about 4 small) ripe yellow peaches, pitted and roughly chopped

⅔ to ¾ cup agave nectar

1 teaspoon fresh lemon juice

½ teaspoon orange-flower water (optional)

This is a wonderful sorbet for summer, when farmers' markets are teeming with a variety of peaches. I prefer to leave the skins on for their added specks of bright color. A small splash of orange-flower water boosts the peaches' natural floral flavor. Process the sorbet immediately after mixing to preserve the fruit's fresh taste. It is best served straight from the ice cream maker, or at least on the same day.

Blend the peaches, ⅔ cup agave nectar, and the lemon juice in a blender or food processor until the mixture is completely smooth. Taste the puree and add the additional agave if you wish it to be sweeter. (The sorbet will taste a little less sweet after it is frozen.) Stir in the orange-flower water, if using.

Process the sorbet in an ice cream machine according to the manufacturer's directions until it is firm. Serve immediately.

# Double-Chocolate Brownies

MAKES 16 BROWNIES

PER BROWNIE: 130 CALORIES, 8 GRAMS FAT

Nonstick pan spray

½ cup plus 2 tablespoons all-purpose flour

½ teaspoon salt

3 tablespoons canola oil

¾ cup sugar

⅓ cup plain nonfat Greek-style yogurt

1 teaspoon pure vanilla extract

½ cup unsweetened Dutch-processed cocoa powder

2 egg whites from large eggs

⅓ cup mini semisweet chocolate chips

**Even the most discerning brownie connoisseur will delight in the rich, chocolatey taste of these. Most of the flavor comes from the cocoa powder, so choose a brand with great flavor, such as Guittard or Wondercocoa. Miniature chocolate chips ensure plenty of morsels in every bite. Leaving the brownies slightly underbaked is the key to keeping them moist and fudgy.**

Preheat the oven to 350°F with a rack in the center position. Coat a 9-inch square baking pan with pan spray.

In a small bowl, whisk together the flour and salt; set aside.

Heat the oil in a medium saucepan over medium heat just until warm. Use a whisk to stir in the sugar until it is evenly moistened. Add the yogurt and vanilla, and stir until thoroughly combined. Stir in the cocoa powder, several tablespoons at a time, to make a thick, dark paste.

In a small clean bowl and using a clean whisk, beat the egg whites just until they are very thick and foamy. Whisk the whites into the chocolate mixture just to combine. Fold in the flour mixture until streaky, then fold in the chocolate chips just until combined.

Spread the batter evenly in the prepared pan. Bake for 15 minutes, or until the top has formed a crust and a knife inserted into the center still comes out with wet crumbs on it. Transfer the pan to a wire rack and let it cool for at least 1 hour before cutting.

To serve: Cut the brownies into 4 even strips one way, then 4 the other, to make 16 brownies.

Store any leftover brownies at room temperature, tightly wrapped in plastic film, for up to 4 days, or overwrap with foil and freeze for up to 2 weeks. Thaw individual frozen brownies at room temperature.

# Exotic Hot Chocolate

3 tablespoons sugar

2½ tablespoons unsweetened Dutch-processed cocoa powder

⅛ teaspoon ground cinnamon

⅛ teaspoon cayenne pepper

1½ cups nonfat or 1% milk

½ vanilla bean

Scant ¼ cup semisweet or bittersweet chocolate chips

2 tablespoons rosewater, or to taste

2 or 3 small cinnamon sticks (optional)

SWEET & SUGAR FREE!

Replace the sugar with 1 tablespoon plus 2 teaspoons (6 packets) of Truvía and substitute chopped unsweetened chocolate for the chocolate chips. Start with 1 tablespoon of the rosewater and add more to taste.

Spiced with cinnamon and cayenne and scented with rosewater, this is the perfect hot chocolate to warm up with on a cold day. I first tasted the combination of chocolate and rosewater on a chilly day in Colorado, where I was participating in the annual *Bon Appétit* Culinary Festival. When I returned home, I began to play with the magical combination, building on the layers of flavor with spices while cutting out the cream. Look for rosewater in the international aisle of your supermarket.

In a small saucepan, stir together the sugar, cocoa powder, cinnamon, and cayenne. Whisk in the milk and ½ cup water.

Use a paring knife to slit the vanilla bean lengthwise and scrape the seeds into the saucepan. Toss in the pod, too.

Bring the mixture to a boil over medium heat, whisking frequently and scraping along the bottom of the saucepan to prevent sticking. As soon as the mixture boils, remove the saucepan from the heat and add the chocolate chips and the rosewater. Pull out the vanilla pod and discard it, or rinse and reserve it for another use.

Let the hot chocolate stand for 1 minute to allow the chocolate to melt, then whisk it smooth.

*To serve:* Divide the hot chocolate among two or three small (4- to 6-ounce) sake or tea cups and serve piping hot, garnished with the cinnamon sticks, if desired.

# Apricot Bars

PER BAR: 210 CALORIES, 4 GRAMS FAT

Nonstick pan spray

2 cups dried apricots

1 cup apricot jam

1 teaspoon fresh lemon juice

1 cup all-purpose flour

¾ cup (packed) dark brown sugar

⅓ cup plus 1 tablespoon rolled oats

1 teaspoon finely grated lemon zest

¼ teaspoon ground cinnamon

¼ teaspoon ground ginger

¼ teaspoon salt

3 ounces (6 tablespoons) reduced-fat cream cheese (neufchâtel), preferably Kraft brand, cold, cut into ¼-inch cubes

¼ cup (½ stick) unsalted butter, cold, cut into ¼-inch cubes

**These healthy bars make a sweet-tooth-satisfying snack. They freeze well and are perfect for toting to the gym, taking on hikes or camping trips, packing in the kids' lunch boxes, or carrying to work for a midday pick-me-up. The dried apricots are full of nutrients and the jam does double duty, sweetening the bars while boosting the apricot flavor.**

Preheat the oven to 350°F with a rack in the center position. Coat a 9-inch square baking pan with pan spray.

Roughly chop the apricots into approximately ¾-inch pieces. Put them into a small saucepan and add ⅔ cup water. Cook over medium heat for about 5 minutes, until most of the water has been absorbed. Remove from the heat and stir in the jam and lemon juice. Set aside.

In a medium bowl, stir together the flour, brown sugar, oats, lemon zest, cinnamon, ginger, and salt. Add the cream cheese and butter to the flour mixture, and use a pastry cutter or two knives to cut them in until they are in pea-size pieces and the mixture has a crumbly texture. (Alternatively, cut in the cream cheese and butter using a standing mixer fitted with the paddle attachment on medium speed.)

Set aside 1 cup plus 2 tablespoons of the flour mixture in a small bowl. Add 2 to 3 teaspoons cold water to the remaining mixture, and mix just until it forms a dough. (See Make Ahead! note.)

Using your fingers, press the dough into the prepared pan to evenly cover the bottom. If the dough is too sticky to press, cover it with plastic film and press with your fingertips or the flat bottom of a glass; remove the film before baking.

recipe continues

MAKE AHEAD!

Freeze the dough and flour mixture in separate containers for up to 1 week. Thaw in the refrigerator overnight before pressing the dough into the pan. Bake and fill the bars as instructed here.

Bake the crust for 20 minutes, or until it is cooked through but not colored.

Immediately pour the apricot filling over the crust and use a spatula to spread it evenly. Sprinkle the reserved flour mixture evenly over the filling.

Return the pan to the oven for 30 to 35 minutes, until the topping is golden brown. Let the bars cool in the pan on a wire rack for several hours before cutting.

*To serve:* Cut the bars into 4 even strips in one direction, then 4 in the other, to make 16 bars.

Store any leftover bars at room temperature, tightly wrapped, for up to 5 days.

# Tangy Frozen Yogurt

PER SERVING: 150 CALORIES, 0 GRAMS FAT

1 cup plus 2 tablespoons plain nonfat Greek-style yogurt

3 tablespoons agave nectar

1 tablespoon fresh lemon juice

Frozen yogurt that really tastes like yogurt has become wildly popular. Unfortunately, most versions are made with powdered yogurt. The equivalent of a knock-off designer handbag, it isn't as good as the real thing. The solution? Make it yourself, using good-quality yogurt. This easy-to-prepare dessert is superb on its own or dressed up with fresh fruit.

In a medium bowl, whisk together the yogurt, agave nectar, and lemon juice until the mixture is smooth. Freeze in an ice cream machine, according to the manufacturer's directions, letting the machine run for 20 to 30 minutes to make the yogurt as firm as possible.

To serve: Scoop the yogurt into one or two bowls and serve immediately.

Matcha Green Tea Frozen Yogurt Add 1 teaspoon matcha tea powder (available in health food stores and Asian markets) to the yogurt along with the other ingredients.

# Bombay Blondies

Nonstick pan spray

¾ cup plus 1 tablespoon all-purpose flour

2 tablespoons unsweetened shredded coconut

¾ teaspoon curry powder (optional)

½ teaspoon baking powder

¼ teaspoon baking soda

¼ teaspoon salt

3 ounces (6 tablespoons) reduced-fat cream cheese (neufchâtel)

¾ cup (packed) dark brown sugar

1 egg white from a large egg, or 3 tablespoons liquid egg whites

1 teaspoon pure vanilla extract

4 Medjool dates, pitted and finely chopped

¼ cup chopped pecans

This recipe was inspired by the bazaars of Bombay. These days, India's largest city, now called Mumbai, may be known more for "Bollywood" than for its street markets. But if you visit, you would not want to miss the outdoor markets that line the city's streets and dot its narrow alleyways, offering brightly colored baskets of aromatic spices and spice blends, as well as dried fruits like coconut and dates. To make a Bombay Sundae, top each blondie wedge with a scoop of Vanilla Ice Cream (page 37) and a tablespoon of Caramel Sauce (page 32).

Preheat the oven to 350°F with a rack in the center position. Spray an 8-inch round baking pan with pan spray.

In a medium bowl, stir together the flour, coconut, curry powder (if using), baking powder, baking soda, and salt.

In another medium bowl, using an electric mixer, beat the cream cheese and brown sugar on medium speed until the mixture is creamy and free of lumps, about 2 minutes. (If using a standing mixer, use the paddle attachment.) Add the egg white and vanilla, and beat for 1 minute longer. Add the flour mixture on low speed, just until combined. Stir in the dates.

Spread the batter evenly in the prepared pan and sprinkle the pecans on top. Bake for about 20 minutes, until a toothpick inserted into the center comes out clean. Transfer the pan to a wire rack and let the blondies cool, about 30 minutes.

To serve: Cut the blondies into 8 wedges with a sharp knife.

Store any leftovers, tightly wrapped, at room temperature for up to 3 days.

# Pecan Sticky-Bun Coffee Cake

SERVES 12

PER SERVING: 230 CALORIES, 6 GRAMS FAT

Nonstick pan spray

## topping

¾ cup plus 1 tablespoon (packed) dark brown sugar

¾ teaspoon ground cinnamon

⅛ teaspoon salt

1 tablespoon dark corn syrup or brown rice syrup

⅔ cup coarsely chopped pecans

## cake

1½ cups all-purpose flour

½ teaspoon baking powder

½ teaspoon baking soda

½ teaspoon salt

¼ teaspoon ground cinnamon

⅓ cup 2% milk

⅓ cup plain nonfat Greek-style yogurt

1 teaspoon pure vanilla extract

3 ounces (6 tablespoons) reduced-fat cream cheese (neufchâtel)

⅔ cup granulated sugar

½ cup liquid egg substitute

Breakfast for dessert is all the rage, and the sticky bun—with its rich brown sugar coating, hint of cinnamon, and crunchy pecans—has proven to be as much a hit on dessert menus as it is at the breakfast table. With this coffee cake, you get great sticky-bun flavor with a fraction of the fat and a lot less time in the kitchen!

Preheat the oven to 350°F with a rack in the center position. Thoroughly coat a 9-inch round cake pan with pan spray. (Avoid using a springform pan for this cake, because the topping will leak out of the seam.)

To make the topping: In a small bowl, stir together the brown sugar, cinnamon, and salt. Stir in the corn syrup and 1 tablespoon water, and stir for 1 minute to thoroughly moisten the sugar. Stir in the pecans. Put the topping into the prepared pan and use your fingers to press and spread it to evenly cover the bottom.

To make the cake: In a small bowl, whisk together the flour, baking powder, baking soda, salt, and cinnamon. In a separate small bowl, whisk together the milk, yogurt, and vanilla. Set both bowls aside.

In a medium bowl, using an electric mixer, beat the cream cheese and sugar on medium speed for 3 minutes, until well blended and free of lumps. (If using a standing mixer, use the paddle attachment.) Scrape down the bowl with a spatula and add the egg substitute, beating for 1 minute longer.

recipe continues

SERVING
TIP

For a special finish, the cake is
delicious served with the blackberry topping shown on page 167.

Sift half of the flour mixture over the cream cheese mixture, and use a rubber spatula to fold it in. When it becomes just a little streaky, fold in all of the yogurt mixture, just until incorporated. Sift the remaining flour mixture over the batter and fold it in just until the flour is incorporated. Leaving a few lumps is better than overmixing, which will toughen the cake.

Spoon the thick batter over the topping in the pan in five big dollops—one in the center and one near each of the four corners. Gently spread the batter to evenly cover the topping, disturbing it as little as possible.

Bake for 35 to 40 minutes, until a knife inserted into the center of the cake (but not into the topping) comes out clean.

Let the cake cool in the pan on a wire rack for 5 minutes. Invert a serving plate over the pan, and using oven mitts to hold the pan and plate tightly together, flip them over. Pull off the pan to release the cake. Scrape any topping remaining in the pan onto the cake. Let the cake cool for another 20 minutes.

To serve: Cut the cake into 12 wedges and serve warm, or let cool completely and serve at room temperature.

Cover and store any leftovers at room temperature for up to 3 days.

# Banana-Walnut Bread

## SERVES 12

### PER SERVING: 250 CALORIES, 6 GRAMS FAT

Nonstick pan spray

1½ cups all-purpose flour

½ cup whole wheat flour

1 teaspoon baking soda

¼ teaspoon salt

4 very ripe medium bananas

1 teaspoon pure vanilla extract

¼ cup Browned Butter (page 24), or ¼ cup (½ stick) unsalted butter, softened

2 ounces (¼ cup) reduced-fat cream cheese (neufchâtel)

1 cup (packed) dark brown sugar

½ cup liquid egg substitute

¼ cup chopped walnuts (optional)

**MAKE AHEAD!**

The banana bread can be made up to 4 days in advance. Store at room temperature, tightly wrapped, or overwrap with aluminum foil and freeze for up to 2 weeks.

**Banana bread is the perfect way to use up those bananas that have gone past their prime. I collect peeled overripe bananas in a resealable plastic bag in the freezer until I have four, at which point it's time for banana bread!**

Preheat the oven to 350°F with a rack in the center position. Coat an 8 × 4-inch loaf pan with pan spray.

In a small bowl, whisk together the all-purpose and whole wheat flours, baking soda, and salt. In another small bowl, mash the bananas with a fork until they are mostly pureed, with some small pieces remaining. Stir in the vanilla. Set the bowls aside.

In a medium bowl, using an electric mixer, beat the butter, cream cheese, and brown sugar on medium speed for 2 minutes, until light and fluffy. (If using a standing mixer, use the paddle attachment.) Add half of the egg substitute and mix for 1 minute, until well blended. Add the rest of the egg substitute and mix for 1 minute. Add the bananas and mix until combined. Add the flour mixture on low speed just until it is combined.

Using a rubber spatula, spread the batter evenly in the prepared pan. Sprinkle the walnuts over the top, if you are using them.

Bake for 30 minutes. Then rotate the pan from front to back and bake for another 30 minutes, or until a knife inserted into the center comes out with just a few crumbs clinging to it. If the banana bread threatens to brown too much before it is done, tent the top with aluminum foil.

Use oven mitts to invert the banana bread onto a wire rack, and let it cool completely.

To serve: Cut into 12 slices.

# dinner party showstoppers

These special-occasion desserts, developed throughout my years as a pastry chef, are proven crowd-pleasers. Many of these desserts can be prepared as individual portions, which makes them perfect for a dinner party. Some are more exotic, such as the Cornmeal Cakes with Sage and Blackberries, while others, such as the Individual Walnut Cakes with Thyme Syrup and Orange, reflect a culture's traditional cuisine. Then there are my versions of the classics, like Individual S'more Tarts with a chocolatey filling and toasted marshmallow topping. The one element all the desserts in this chapter have in common is their ability to impress and amaze guests. These desserts truly are showstoppers. They are still simple to make, are every bit as good as a restaurant-worthy dessert, and are blissfully low in fat and calories.

# Buttermilk Panna Cotta with Berries

SERVES 4

PER SERVING: 140 CALORIES, 1.5 GRAMS FAT

PER SERVING (SUGAR FREE): 80 CALORIES, 1.5 GRAMS FAT

## panna cotta

¾ cup 2% or whole milk

1¼ teaspoons unflavored gelatin powder

¼ cup sugar

¾ cup low-fat buttermilk, at room temperature

## berry medley

2 tablespoons sugar

¼ vanilla bean

1½ cups mixed berries, such as raspberries, blueberries, and strawberries, large berries quartered

MAKE AHEAD!

The panna cottas can be made up to a day ahead and refrigerated, covered.

SWEET & SUGAR FREE!

Substitute 1¾ tablespoons (5 packets) of Truvía for the sugar in the panna cotta. Substitute 2¼ teaspoons (3 packets) of Truvía for the sugar in the berries.

*Panna cotta* is Italian for "cooked cream." This simple dessert is cooked on the stovetop and thickened with just a small amount of gelatin. Topped with vanilla-scented berries, it is a surefire hit!

To make the panna cotta: Pour the milk into a small saucepan and sprinkle the gelatin evenly over the top. Whisk to combine, then set aside for 3 minutes to soften the gelatin. Whisk in the sugar.

Place the saucepan over medium heat and whisk frequently until the milk begins to steam and the gelatin dissolves completely. Do not allow the mixture to fully boil. Remove the saucepan from the heat and let it cool for 15 minutes. Whisk in the buttermilk.

Pour the mixture into four 4-ounce ramekins. Cover with plastic film and refrigerate for about 3 hours, until it is set.

To prepare the berries: Just before serving, put the sugar in a bowl that is large enough to hold the berries. Use a paring knife to slit the vanilla bean lengthwise and scrape the seeds into the sugar. Rub the seeds into the sugar with your fingertips. Add the berries and mix gently with a spoon or your hands for about 1 minute, until they are well coated and are beginning to release their juices.

To serve: Distribute the berries and their juices evenly over the tops of the panna cottas, and serve.

# Yogurt Mousse with Apricot Coulis

SERVES 6

PER SERVING: 160 CALORIES, 0 GRAMS FAT

## mousse

3 ounces (6 tablespoons) fat-free evaporated milk

½ teaspoon unflavored gelatin powder

⅔ cup plain nonfat Greek-style yogurt

2 tablespoons sugar

1 tablespoon finely grated lemon zest

1 tablespoon fresh lemon juice

## coulis

10 very ripe, large apricots (about 2 pounds), pitted

⅓ cup sugar

¼ cup fresh orange juice

1 tablespoon fresh lemon juice

6 sprigs fresh mint, for garnish

This dessert was inspired by fragrant apricots I found at a farmers' market while working as an assistant pastry chef years ago. The coulis is a simple puree of the fruit, and it bursts with ripe apricot flavor. I enjoy a bit of texture in the sauce, but you can strain it to make it silky smooth if you prefer. Ripe peaches or mangos also work well in place of the apricots. Peel, pit, and cut mangos into chunks before cooking them; no need to peel the apricots or peaches.

To make the mousse: In a small saucepan, whisk together the evaporated milk and the gelatin; let stand for 3 minutes to soften. Warm the mixture over medium heat, stirring, until the gelatin dissolves completely. It will no longer look grainy, and a bit of the hot milk rubbed between your fingers will feel smooth. Transfer the mixture to a medium bowl and freeze it for 10 to 15 minutes, until it is very cold and beginning to gel around the edges.

Whisk together the yogurt, sugar, lemon zest, and lemon juice in a small bowl.

Beat the chilled milk with an electric mixer on medium-high speed for about 2 minutes, until it is very thick and light and holds a medium peak with a curved shape when you lift the beaters. Use a whisk to gently fold in the yogurt mixture.

Spoon the mousse into six 8- to 12-ounce wineglasses or dessert goblets, filling them almost halfway and smoothing the tops. Cover the glasses with plastic film and refrigerate until the mousse is set, about 45 minutes.

MAKE
AHEAD!

Refrigerate the assembled desserts, covered, up to 4 hours
ahead. Or refrigerate the mousse
and coulis separately, covered, for
up to 1 day; spoon the coulis over
the mousse just before serving.
Add the mint immediately before
serving.

*To make the coulis:* Pulse the apricots a few times in a blender or
food processor to roughly chop them. Transfer the fruit to a medium
saucepan and stir in the sugar, orange juice, and lemon juice. Cook
over medium heat, stirring, for 3 minutes, or until the sugar dissolves
and the mixture begins to simmer. Return the fruit to the blender and
puree until it is completely smooth, or leave a little texture if you prefer. Refrigerate until cold, about 1 hour.

*To serve:* Spoon the coulis over the mousse and garnish each dessert
with a sprig of mint.

# Orange Blossom Phyllo Pie

PER SERVING: 170 CALORIES, 6 GRAMS FAT

## syrup

⅔ cup sugar

¼ lemon

2 tablespoons orange-flower
water

## custard

1 vanilla bean

2⅓ cups 2% milk

Pinch of salt

½ teaspoon finely grated orange
zest

¼ teaspoon finely grated lemon
zest

1 large egg

1 egg white from a large egg

½ cup sugar

¼ cup farina or Cream of Wheat
cereal

Nonstick pan spray

7 sheets phyllo, thawed if frozen

4 to 5 tablespoons Browned
Butter (page 24), melted

Milk pie, or *galaktoboureko,* is a staple in Greek pastry shops. The phyllo pie is filled with creamy custard, baked until it is golden and crisp, and then topped with an orange-scented syrup. I have flavored this simple and delicious pastry with the delicate scent of citrus, vanilla, and orange-flower water, which can be found in the international aisle in most supermarkets.

To make the syrup: In a small, nonreactive saucepan, mix the sugar with ½ cup water. Squeeze 1 teaspoon juice from the lemon into the pan, and drop in the lemon quarter as well. Bring the mixture to a boil over medium heat and boil for 5 minutes, or until it is slightly thickened. Remove from the heat and let cool to room temperature, about 1 hour. Remove the lemon quarter and stir in the orange-flower water. Set aside.

To make the custard: Use a paring knife to slit the vanilla bean lengthwise and scrape the seeds into a small saucepan. Stir in 2 cups of the milk and bring to a boil. Remove the pan from the heat, and whisk in the salt, orange zest, and lemon zest. Set aside to cool.

Using an electric mixer, beat the egg and egg white on high speed until they are foamy. Gradually add the sugar, a few teaspoons at a time. Whisk in the farina, then the cooled milk.

Transfer the mixture to a medium saucepan and cook over medium heat for about 5 minutes, until it is slightly thickened. Set aside.

*recipe continues*

MAKE
AHEAD!

The syrup can be made up to
1 week ahead and refrigerated in
an airtight container.

WORKING
WITH
PHYLLO

Phyllo is a paper-thin pastry that
dries out very easily. Work quickly,
keeping the reserved sheets covered with a damp towel as you
work.

*To assemble:* Preheat the oven to 375°F with a rack in the center position. Coat a 9-inch round cake pan with pan spray.

Place 1 sheet of phyllo in the bottom of the prepared pan, running straight top to bottom as you face the pan (12 o'clock to 6 o'clock), letting the ends drape over the sides of the pan. Use a pastry brush to coat the sheet with melted butter. Place the second layer of phyllo at a slight angle to the first (1 o'clock to 7 o'clock), and brush with butter. Repeat with 3 more layers, rotating each layer "one hour" and brushing each with butter, to cover the entire pan.

Whisk the remaining ⅓ cup milk into the custard, then pour the custard into the phyllo-lined pan. Fold all the overhanging pieces of phyllo over the custard, brushing each layer with melted butter as you lay it down. Cut the final 2 pieces of phyllo in half with a sharp knife. Brush each piece with butter, gather the pieces together, and arrange them loosely on top of the pie like crumpled pieces of paper.

*To finish:* Bake for 35 to 45 minutes, until golden brown. Transfer the pan to a wire rack and immediately pour the syrup evenly over the top of the pie. Let cool, uncovered, at room temperature for several hours before cutting.

*To serve:* Cut the pie into 12 wedges.

Refrigerate any leftover pie, tightly covered, for up to 2 days.

# Butterscotch Pudding

SERVES 5 OR 6

PER SERVING: 190 CALORIES, 7 GRAMS FAT

½ cup plus 2 tablespoons liquid egg substitute

2 tablespoons cornstarch

1 teaspoon pure vanilla extract

Pinch of salt

1 cup 2% milk

½ cup whole milk

⅓ cup (packed) dark brown sugar

⅓ cup butterscotch chips

1½ teaspoons Browned Butter (page 24), softened

Luscious Whipped Topping (page 35) or store-bought whipped topping, for garnish (optional)

MAKE AHEAD!

Refrigerate the pudding in a large bowl or in individual ramekins up to 4 days ahead. Once the pudding is completely cool, press plastic film directly onto the surface to prevent a skin from forming.

Ever since I was a child, butterscotch pudding has been one of my favorite comfort-food desserts. I've used Browned Butter (page 24) and added butterscotch chips to boost the flavor while using very little butter. The result tastes just like the one I remember from childhood.

In a medium bowl, whisk the egg substitute, cornstarch, vanilla, and salt until combined; set aside.

In a medium saucepan, whisk the 2% milk, whole milk, and brown sugar over medium heat until the milk begins to steam. Use a heat-proof spatula to stir in the butterscotch chips, pressing them against the sides and bottom of the pan until they are completely melted and the mixture is smooth.

Add the hot milk mixture to the eggs in a slow stream, whisking constantly. Pour the whole thing back into the saucepan and cook over medium heat for about 3 minutes, whisking frequently, until the mixture thickens to a pudding consistency.

Strain the pudding through a fine-mesh strainer into a clean medium bowl, and whisk in the browned butter until it melts in. Cover the bowl with plastic film and refrigerate for several hours, until cold.

*To serve:* Spoon ⅓ to ½ cup of the pudding into individual ramekins or dessert bowls. Garnish with a dollop of topping, if desired.

# Rosemary Angel Food Cake with Lemon Glaze

SERVES 12

PER SERVING: 200 CALORIES, 0 GRAMS FAT

## angel food cake

1½ cups egg whites (from about 12 large eggs), at room temperature

1½ teaspoons cream of tartar

¼ teaspoon salt

1½ cups granulated sugar

1 tablespoon finely chopped fresh rosemary

½ teaspoon pure vanilla extract

½ teaspoon pure almond extract

1½ cups cake flour, sifted

## lemon glaze

½ cup powdered sugar

½ teaspoon finely grated lemon zest

1 tablespoon fresh lemon juice

Angel food cake was my slumber-party cake as a child. When friends spent the night, we would head for the kitchen in our PJs to bake. Ignorant of its health benefits, we loved angel food cake for its mixing, for the way it climbed up the sides of the tube pan as it baked, and because it stayed so pristinely white. In this recipe, angel food cake gets a modern-day makeover with fresh herbs and a sweet-tart lemon glaze. This quick and easy cake is perfect for dinner parties—and grown-up slumber parties, too.

To make the cake: Preheat the oven to 325°F with a rack in the center position.

Using a standing mixer fitted with the whisk attachment, beat the egg whites on high speed until they are foamy. (Alternatively, use a hand-held electric mixer.) Add the cream of tartar and the salt. With the mixer still on high, gradually add the sugar, a few teaspoons at a time. After all of the sugar is in, continue to mix until soft, glossy peaks form, curling over gently when you lift the beater. Mix in the rosemary and the vanilla and almond extracts just until everything is combined.

Sift one-third of the flour over the meringue, and fold it in with a spatula until it is mostly incorporated. Repeat twice more until the flour is completely incorporated.

Spread the batter evenly in an ungreased 10-inch angel food cake pan. Bake for 20 minutes. Raise the temperature to 350°F and bake for 20 minutes longer, until the top is light golden, the cake springs back

recipe continues

**MAKE AHEAD!**

The unglazed cake can be made up to 1 day in advance and stored, tightly wrapped, at room temperature.

when lightly pressed with your finger, and a cake tester inserted into the cake comes out clean. Set the pan on a wire rack to cool for 5 minutes. Remove the cake from the pan and transfer it directly to the rack to cool completely, about 2 hours.

*To make the glaze:* Sift the powdered sugar into a small bowl and whisk in the lemon zest and juice until the mixture is smooth. Cover and set aside.

*To finish:* Set the cooled cake on a serving plate and spoon the glaze over the top. Use the back of the spoon to spread the glaze over the top of the cake, allowing some to drip down the sides. Let the glaze set for at least 30 minutes.

*To serve:* Cut the cake into 12 pieces with a serrated knife, using a gentle sawing motion.

Store any leftover cake, tightly wrapped, at room temperature for up to 4 days.

# Orange Soufflé Cake with Strawberry-Basil Salad

SERVES 12

PER SERVING: 190 CALORIES, 4 GRAMS FAT

## cake

Nonstick pan spray

¾ cup sifted cake flour, plus more for coating the pan

½ cup plus ⅔ cup sugar

⅛ teaspoon salt

⅔ cup low-fat buttermilk

Finely grated zest of 1 orange

Finely grated zest of ½ lemon

¼ cup fresh orange juice

2 tablespoons fresh lemon juice

1½ tablespoons extra virgin olive oil

6 egg whites from large eggs

### MAKE AHEAD!

Store the strawberry-basil salad—minus the basil—at room temperature, covered, for up to 2 hours in advance. Sliver and add the basil just before serving.

This cake combines the best qualities of two desserts: light like a soufflé, yet moist and substantial like a cake. I love the way the lemon-infused oil brightens the strawberries. My favorite is Olave Limón olive oil (see Sources & Resources on page 236). This cake is best when served on the day it is made.

To make the cake: Preheat the oven to 350°F with a rack in the center position. Coat a 9-inch springform pan with pan spray and dust it lightly with cake flour, knocking out any excess.

In a medium bowl, whisk together the cake flour, the ½ cup sugar, and the salt. Stir in the buttermilk, orange and lemon zests, orange and lemon juices, and olive oil just until no lumps of flour remain.

Use an electric mixer to beat the egg whites on high speed until foamy. Add the ⅔ cup sugar in a slow, steady stream as you continue to beat the whites. After all of the sugar is in, continue to beat until the whites form medium peaks that hold a curved shape when you lift the beater.

Gently fold the flour mixture into the egg whites until the mixture is no longer streaky. Pour the batter into the prepared pan and bake for about 25 minutes, until the top is light golden and a toothpick inserted into the center comes out clean.

Transfer the cake to a wire rack and let it cool completely, about 1½ hours. Then unlatch and remove the sides of the pan and transfer the cake, on the base, to a serving plate.

## strawberry-basil salad

3 cups strawberries, hulled and quartered

3 tablespoons sugar

1½ tablespoons lemon olive oil, or ½ teaspoon finely grated lemon zest mixed into 1½ tablespoons extra virgin olive oil

12 medium to large fresh basil leaves, plus 12 sprigs fresh basil for garnish

To make the strawberry-basil salad: In a medium bowl, gently stir the strawberries, sugar, and olive oil for about 1 minute, until the berries begin to release their juices. Stack the basil leaves on a cutting board, roll them up tightly the long way, and cut crosswise into thin slices to make a chiffonade. Stir the chiffonade into the berries.

To serve: Cut the cake into 12 wedges, and serve each wedge with a generous spoonful of the salad, along with some of the juices from the bowl and a sprig of basil.

# Chocolate Peanut Butter Cups

SERVES 4

PER SERVING: 220 CALORIES, 12 GRAMS FAT

Nonstick pan spray

⅓ cup semisweet chocolate chips

1 tablespoon unsalted butter

¼ teaspoon salt

2 tablespoons plain nonfat Greek-style yogurt

1 tablespoon liquid egg substitute

½ teaspoon pure vanilla extract

¼ cup unsweetened Dutch-processed cocoa powder

1 tablespoon all-purpose flour

2 egg whites from large eggs

⅓ cup sugar

4 teaspoons reduced-fat peanut butter, smooth or chunky, preferably natural style

My mother used to make individual chocolate cakes for me and my playmates. Each having our own made us feel extra special. Years later, I dusted off her recipe to prepare for old friends, adding a peanut butter center for a sweet-salty twist.

Preheat the oven to 400°F with a rack in the center position. Coat four 4-ounce ramekins or muffin cups with pan spray. If using ramekins, set them on a rimmed baking sheet.

Melt the chocolate, butter, and 1½ tablespoons water in a double boiler, or in a microwave oven, until you can stir the mixture smooth. Whisk in the salt, yogurt, egg substitute, and vanilla. In a small bowl, stir together the cocoa powder and flour.

Using a standing mixer fitted with the whisk attachment, beat the egg whites on high speed until they are foamy. (Alternatively, use a handheld electric mixer.) With the mixer running, gradually add the sugar, a few teaspoons at a time. After all of the sugar is in, continue to mix until soft, glossy peaks form, curling over when you lift the beater.

Fold the chocolate mixture into the egg whites until mostly combined. Sift half of the cocoa mixture over the top and fold it in with a spatula. Once it is mostly incorporated, sift the remaining cocoa mixture over the top and fold until it is incorporated.

recipe continues

MAKE
AHEAD!

The filled but unbaked cakes can be refrigerated, covered, for up to 3 days before baking. Place in the preheated oven directly from the refrigerator and increase the baking time to 20 minutes.

Spoon ¼ cup of the batter into each prepared ramekin. Place 1 teaspoon of the peanut butter in the center of each one, and cover the peanut butter with a heaping tablespoon of batter.

Bake for 15 minutes, or until a toothpick inserted into the cake (not the center) comes out clean. Set the ramekins on a wire rack and let them cool for several hours.

*To serve:* Serve the cakes in the ramekins. If you used muffin cups, unmold them before serving.

Store any leftover peanut butter cups, tightly wrapped, at room temperature for up to 24 hours.

# Raspberry-Custard Tart

SERVES 12

PER SERVING: 200 CALORIES, 7 GRAMS FAT

## vanilla custard

⅔ cup liquid egg substitute

2 tablespoons plus ½ teaspoon cornstarch

⅛ teaspoon salt

⅓ cup plus 1 tablespoon sugar

1 vanilla bean

1½ cups 2% milk

1 Graham Cracker Pie Crust (page 29), baked in a 10-inch tart pan, cooled to room temperature

18 ounces (about 4½ cups) raspberries

MAKE AHEAD!

Make and refrigerate the custard a day ahead, pressing plastic film directly onto the surface after it is completely cool to prevent a skin from forming. The finished tart can be refrigerated for up to 4 hours before serving.

I love to serve this tart in summer, when raspberries are bright red and juicy. The sweet vanilla custard perfectly complements the berries. This is the ideal dinner party dessert—simple to prepare, beautiful to behold, and delicious to eat.

To make the custard: In a large bowl, whisk together the egg substitute, cornstarch, and salt; set aside.

Put the sugar in a small saucepan. Use a paring knife to slit the vanilla bean lengthwise and scrape the seeds into the pan. Whisk in the milk, then drop in the vanilla pod. Stir the mixture over medium heat until it begins to bubble.

Pour the hot milk into the egg mixture in a slow stream, whisking constantly. Return the mixture to the saucepan and cook over medium-low heat, whisking constantly, for several minutes, until the custard thickens enough to coat the back of a spoon.

Strain the custard through a fine-mesh strainer into a clean bowl. Lightly cover the bowl with plastic film and refrigerate it for 1 to 2 hours, until cool.

To finish: Pour and spread the custard evenly into the crust, and arrange the berries over the top.

To serve: Cut into 12 wedges.

Refrigerate any leftovers, covered, for up to 2 days.

# Pineapple Upside-Down Cake

Nonstick pan spray

## topping

⅔ cup (packed) dark brown sugar

½ small ripe pineapple, peeled, trimmed, and cored

## cake

1½ cups all-purpose flour

2 teaspoons baking powder

¼ teaspoon salt

2 ounces (¼ cup) reduced-fat cream cheese (neufchâtel)

¼ cup Browned Butter (page 24), softened

½ cup granulated sugar

¼ cup (packed) dark brown sugar

2½ tablespoons liquid egg substitute

2 teaspoons pure vanilla extract

½ cup 2% milk, at room temperature

2 egg whites from large eggs

Luscious Whipped Topping (page 35) or store-bought whipped topping, for serving (optional)

Upside-down cakes, or skillet cakes, first appeared in the 1800s, when ovens were not always practical or reliable. During the 1920s, pineapple became the fruit of choice for these inverted cakes, and they have remained a favorite of mine. If you include the whipped topping, try adding a tablespoon or so of dark rum to it. It complements the pineapple perfectly.

Preheat the oven to 350°F with a rack in the center position. Coat a 9-inch round cake pan with pan spray.

*To make the topping:* Sprinkle the brown sugar over the bottom of the prepared pan. Cut the pineapple lengthwise into quarters, lay the quarters cut-side-down, and cut them crosswise into ½-inch-thick slices. Lay the slices in the pan in concentric circles so that they are almost touching. Set the pan aside.

*To make the cake:* Sift the flour, baking powder, and salt into a medium bowl.

Using a standing mixer fitted with the paddle attachment, beat the cream cheese, butter, and granulated and brown sugars on medium speed for 5 minutes. (Alternatively, use a handheld electric mixer.)

In a small bowl, whisk together the egg substitute and vanilla. Add half of the egg mixture, to the cream cheese mixture, and mix for 1 to 2 minutes. Add the remaining egg mixture and mix for 1 minute longer.

Sift one-third of the flour mixture into the cream cheese mixture and gently fold it in by hand. Fold in half of the milk, then sift in another third of the flour. Repeat with the remaining milk and flour, ending with the flour. Set the batter aside.

In a clean bowl using clean beaters, beat the egg whites until they are tripled in volume and hold firm peaks when you lift the beaters. Fold the whites into the batter until it is no longer streaky.

Spread the batter evenly over the pineapple in the pan, taking care not to move the pineapple. Bake for about 35 minutes, until a knife inserted into the center of the cake comes out clean.

Let the cake cool in the pan on a wire rack for 5 minutes. Then invert a serving plate over the pan, carefully grip the pan and plate together with oven mitts, and flip them over to release the cake onto the plate. Lift off the cake pan, transfer any topping in the pan to the cake, and let the cake cool for 2 hours before serving.

To serve: Cut the cake into 10 to 12 wedges, and garnish each one with a dollop of topping, if desired.

Store any leftover cake, tightly covered, at room temperature for up to 1 day.

# Cornmeal Cakes with Sage and Blackberries

## SERVES 12

PER SERVING: 230 CALORIES, 5 GRAMS FAT

### cornmeal cakes

Nonstick pan spray

1½ cups all-purpose flour

¼ cup plus 1 tablespoon yellow cornmeal

2 teaspoons baking powder

¼ teaspoon salt

½ cup plain nonfat Greek-style yogurt

¼ cup 2% milk, at room temperature

1 teaspoon pure vanilla extract

¼ cup Browned Butter (page 24), softened

¾ cup sugar

3 tablespoons liquid egg substitute

1 egg white from a large egg, at room temperature

12 small fresh sage leaves

Baked in muffin pans, these cakes are like a sweet, tender corn bread. Sage gives them a subtle herbal flavor that perfectly complements the blackberries. This is a great dessert for late summer, when berries are at their most flavorful. Toasted leftover cakes make a wonderful breakfast the following morning.

To make the cakes: Preheat the oven to 350°F with a rack in the center position. Coat 12 muffin cups with pan spray.

In a small bowl, whisk together the flour, cornmeal, baking powder, and salt. In another small bowl, whisk together the yogurt, milk, and vanilla. Set both bowls aside.

Using an electric mixer, beat the butter and sugar on medium speed for 2 minutes. Add the liquid egg substitute and beat for another 3 minutes, until the mixture is light and fluffy. By hand, stir in one-third of the flour mixture, then half of the yogurt mixture, half of the remaining flour mixture, all of the remaining yogurt mixture, and all of the remaining flour mixture. Each time, stir just long enough to combine the ingredients.

In a clean medium bowl with clean beaters, beat the egg white on high speed until soft peaks form, curling over softly when you lift the beaters. Fold the egg white into the cake batter.

recipe continues

## blackberry topping

6 cups blackberries

2 teaspoons kirsch (optional)

¼ cup plus 2 tablespoons sugar

Luscious Whipped Topping (page 35) or store-bought whipped topping, for serving (optional)

Spoon the batter evenly into the prepared muffin cups. Drape a sage leaf over the center of each cake. Bake for 20 minutes, or until the edges are light golden and a toothpick inserted into the center comes out clean.

Let the cakes cool in the muffin pan for at least 2 hours.

*To make the blackberry topping:* Put 2 cups of the berries into a medium bowl. Add the kirsch, if using, and mash the berries slightly with a fork to release some of their juices. Add the sugar and the remaining 4 cups berries, stirring until the mixture is saucelike.

*To serve:* Serve the cornmeal cakes on individual dessert plates with ½ cup of the berries to one side. Top the berries with a spoonful of whipped topping, if desired.

Store any leftover cakes, tightly wrapped, at room temperature for up to 2 days, or freeze for up to 2 weeks; thaw at room temperature overnight. Refrigerate any leftover topping, tightly covered, for up to 24 hours.

# Rhubarb Crisp
# with Pine Nut Streusel Topping

SERVES 6

PER SERVING: 240 CALORIES, 8 GRAMS FAT
PER SERVING (SUGAR FREE): 140 CALORIES, 8 GRAMS FAT

## topping

¼ cup (½ stick) unsalted butter, cold

1½ ounces (3 tablespoons) reduced-fat cream cheese (neufchâtel), preferably Kraft brand, cold

¾ cup all-purpose flour

⅓ cup (packed) dark brown sugar

2 tablespoons pine nuts

1 teaspoon pure vanilla extract

1 teaspoon finely grated lemon zest

¼ teaspoon ground cinnamon

¼ teaspoon ground ginger

¼ teaspoon ground nutmeg

¼ teaspoon salt

MAKE AHEAD!

The topping mixture can be frozen in a resealable plastic bag up to 3 weeks in advance.

Had my mom thought to bake vegetables into a sweet crisp for dessert, she would have had a much easier time getting me to eat my veggies! Although rhubarb is a vegetable, its balanced sweet-tart flavor makes it a perfect dessert choice, particularly in pies and crisps. In this dinner party dessert that makes comfort food upscale, pine nuts in the streusel topping add a sophisticated twist.

To make the topping: Cut the butter and cream cheese into ¼-inch cubes, arrange them in a single layer on a baking sheet, and freeze until they are very firm but not frozen solid, about 20 minutes.

Using a standing mixer fitted with the paddle attachment, mix the flour, brown sugar, pine nuts, vanilla, lemon zest, cinnamon, ginger, nutmeg, and salt on medium-low speed just to combine. Add the chilled butter and cream cheese, and mix on medium speed until they are in small pebble-size pieces. (Alternatively, stir everything except the butter and cream cheese together in a bowl, and then cut in the butter and cream cheese with a pastry cutter or two knives.)

Freeze the topping mixture for 15 minutes.

About 20 minutes before baking, preheat the oven to 375°F with a rack in the center position.

*recipe continues*

## filling

½ cup granulated sugar

2 tablespoons all-purpose flour

⅛ teaspoon ground cinnamon

10 ounces rhubarb, cut into
½-inch pieces (about 3 cups)

Vanilla Ice Cream (page 37)
or Dreyer's Slow Churned
Vanilla Ice Cream, for serving
(optional)

Substitute ½ cup plus 3½ tablespoons (37 packets) of Truvía for
the brown sugar in the topping.
Substitute ¼ cup (15 packets) of
Truvía for the granulated sugar in
the filling.

**To make the filling:** In a medium bowl, stir together the sugar, flour, and cinnamon. Add the rhubarb and toss until it is evenly coated.

**To finish:** Divide the filling evenly among six 6-ounce ramekins or custard cups. Top each with ⅓ cup of the topping. Bake until the topping is golden and the rhubarb is bubbling, about 25 minutes. Let cool for about 20 minutes. Serve warm, topped with ice cream, if desired.

# Pavlovas with Coconut Custard and Passion Fruit

## coconut custard

1½ cups 2% milk

⅓ cup plus 1 tablespoon sugar

⅓ cup plus 1 tablespoon liquid egg substitute

2 tablespoons cornstarch

⅛ teaspoon salt

½ teaspoon pure vanilla extract

½ teaspoon natural coconut extract

¼ cup plus 1 tablespoon sweetened flake coconut, toasted

## meringue shells

4 egg whites from large eggs, at room temperature

¼ teaspoon cream of tartar

¾ cup plus 1 tablespoon sugar

1 teaspoon natural coconut extract

1 large mango

2 kiwi fruits

8 passion fruits

*Food & Wine* featured my recipe for this low-fat dinner-party dessert. The crunchy meringues paired with tropical fruit are not only visually striking—they are an exercise in exciting contrasts: at once soft and crunchy, sweet and tart. This version is even better than the original, with creamy coconut custard adding an extra layer of silky texture and flavor.

To make the custard: In a small saucepan, whisk the milk and sugar over medium heat until the milk begins to steam. Remove from the heat.

In a medium bowl, whisk together the egg substitute, cornstarch, salt, and vanilla and coconut extracts. Gradually whisk in the steaming milk until it is incorporated. Return the mixture to the saucepan and cook over medium heat, whisking constantly, for 1 to 2 minutes, until it is thick enough to coat a spoon.

Strain the custard through a fine-mesh strainer into a medium bowl. Whisk in the toasted coconut. Cover the bowl loosely with plastic film and refrigerate it for at least 5 hours, until the custard is cold.

To make the meringue shells: Preheat the oven to 250°F with one rack in the center position and another in the lower third of the oven. Line two rimmed baking sheets with parchment paper or silicone baking mats.

recipe continues

MAKE
AHEAD!

The custard can be made a day ahead and refrigerated; press plastic film directly onto the surface of the cooled custard to prevent a skin from forming. The meringue shells can be made up to 3 days in advance and stored at room temperature in an airtight container, layered between sheets of waxed paper and kept away from moisture. Fill the shells immediately before serving.

Using a standing mixer fitted with the whisk attachment, beat the egg whites on high speed until they are foamy. (Alternatively, use a handheld electric mixer.) Add the cream of tartar, beating until it is incorporated. With the mixer running, gradually add the sugar, a few teaspoons at a time. After all of the sugar is in, continue to beat until firm, glossy peaks form, standing up without curling over when you lift the beater. Add the coconut extract, beating just until it is incorporated.

Mound 4 meringues on each prepared baking sheet, using about ⅔ cup for each and spacing them evenly, with plenty of space around each mound. Use the back of a spoon to spread each mound into a 3- to 4-inch round. Use the spoon to make a well in the center of each one to hold the filling.

Bake for 40 minutes. Then reduce the temperature to 200°F and bake for an additional 2½ hours. The shells should remain pale but should be dried all the way through. Transfer the sheets to wire racks to cool for 20 minutes. Use a thin spatula to carefully peel the shells from the sheets, and let them cool directly on the racks for another 20 minutes, until they are cooled completely.

To finish: Peel the mango and cut the flesh into ¼-inch-thick slices. Without peeling them, cut the kiwi fruits into ½-inch-thick rounds. Cut the passion fruits in half, taking care that the pulp does not spill out.

To serve: Place the meringue shells on individual plates. Spoon the coconut custard into the centers and top with the fruits.

# Gingerbread Cake with Spiced Apples

## gingerbread cake

Nonstick pan spray

1 cup all-purpose flour

¼ cup whole wheat flour

½ teaspoon ground ginger

½ teaspoon ground cinnamon

¼ teaspoon ground cloves

¼ teaspoon freshly ground black pepper (ground fine)

½ cup chopped Medjool dates

⅔ cup unsweetened applesauce

½ cup (packed) dark brown sugar

⅓ cup unsulfured molasses

⅓ cup canola oil

Scant ¼ cup grated fresh ginger

1 teaspoon baking soda

3 tablespoons liquid egg substitute

This rich cake is wonderfully spicy. Freshly grated ginger is key; scrape the root with the tip of a spoon to easily peel away the skin without losing precious ginger. I prefer Fuji apples in this recipe, as they hold their shape well. Leftover Gingerbread Cake is an indulgent (but low-fat!) substitute for a morning muffin.

To make the cake: Preheat the oven to 350°F with a rack in the center position. Coat a 9-inch round cake pan or springform pan with pan spray.

In a small bowl, whisk together the all-purpose and whole wheat flours, ground ginger, cinnamon, cloves, and black pepper; set aside.

Put the dates in a small bowl and pour ½ cup hot water over them; let stand for 5 minutes.

In a food processor, pulse the applesauce, brown sugar, molasses, oil, and fresh ginger (including any juices from grating) to combine. Add the dates and any water remaining in the bowl, and process for 30 seconds, or until the dates are pureed, scraping down the sides as needed.

Transfer the mixture to a medium bowl and whisk in the baking soda, then the liquid egg substitute, and finally the flour mixture, mixing each time just until the mixture is well combined.

Pour the batter into the prepared pan and bake for 30 to 35 minutes, until a knife inserted into the center comes out clean. Let the cake cool in the pan on a rack for 45 minutes. Run a knife around the edges of the pan, transfer the cake directly to the rack, and let it cool completely.

recipe continues

## spiced apples

¼ cup plus 1 tablespoon granulated sugar

4 firm medium apples, such as Fuji, peeled, cored, and cut into ½-inch dice

½ teaspoon ground cinnamon

2 tablespoons brandy

2 tablespoons fresh orange juice

Luscious Whipped Topping (page 35), Vanilla Ice Cream (page 37), or Dreyer's Slow Churned Vanilla Ice Cream, for serving (optional)

*To make the spiced apples:* In a skillet, stir the sugar with ½ cup water over medium-high heat until the mixture boils. Add the apples and cinnamon, and cook, stirring frequently, for 5 minutes, or until the apples are crisp-tender. Add the brandy, and using a flameproof oven mitt, tilt the skillet away from yourself and carefully light the liquid in the skillet using the flame from the stove, a match, or a lighter. Cook for 1 minute to burn off the alcohol. Stir in the orange juice. Remove the skillet from the heat.

*To serve:* Cut the cake into 12 wedges. Cut one wedge into 2 layers, and arrange them on a plate by leaning the top piece against the bottom one. Spoon ¼ cup of the apple topping beside the cake. Repeat with the remaining wedges and spiced apples. Top with whipped topping or ice cream, if desired.

Store any leftover cake, tightly wrapped, at room temperature for 2 to 3 days. Refrigerate any leftover spiced apples in an airtight container for up to 2 days.

# Individual S'more Tarts

PER SERVING (½ TART): 245 CALORIES, 8 GRAMS FAT

## custard

⅔ cup liquid egg substitute

2 tablespoons plus 1 teaspoon cornstarch

⅓ cup plus 1 tablespoon sugar

1 tablespoon good-quality unsweetened cocoa powder, Dutch-processed or natural

¼ teaspoon salt

1½ cups 2% milk

¼ cup semisweet chocolate chips, melted

## crust

1 Graham Cracker Pie Crust (page 29), formed in six 4½-inch tart shells with removable bottoms and baked

## marshmallow topping

2¼ teaspoons unflavored gelatin powder

½ cup plus 1 tablespoon sugar

⅓ cup egg whites (from about 3 large eggs)

½ teaspoon pure vanilla extract

When I was a kid, my dad would occasionally take me out on his boat on Lake Powell, a seemingly endless reservoir straddling the Utah–Arizona border. I don't know which I looked forward to more—playing endlessly in the water or making s'mores over the open fire. This is a sophisticated version of the classic campfire treat. The homemade marshmallow topping is worth the effort, but store-bought marshmallow creme will work in a pinch. The s'mores can also be baked in a 9-inch tart pan.

To make the custard: In a small bowl, whisk the egg substitute and cornstarch together; set aside.

Put the sugar, cocoa powder, and salt into a medium saucepan. Whisk in the milk. Bring to a boil over medium heat, stirring occasionally.

Pour about half of the hot milk mixture into the eggs in a steady stream, whisking constantly to avoid scrambling the eggs. Pour the mixture back into the saucepan and cook for several minutes, stirring constantly, until the custard is thick enough to coat the back of a spoon.

Pour the custard through a fine-mesh strainer into a medium bowl. Whisk in the melted chocolate. Cover the custard with plastic film, poking several holes in the film to allow steam to escape. Refrigerate for several hours, until it is cold.

Fill the baked tart shells with a scant ⅓ cup of custard each, spreading it evenly into the shells. Gently press up on the bottoms of the tart shells to remove the outer pan rings. Set aside.

To make the marshmallow topping: Put the gelatin into a small bowl, add 1½ tablespoons water, and stir gently. Set aside for 5 minutes to soften.

recipe continues

The custard can be refrigerated up to 2 days in advance; press plastic film directly onto the surface of the cooled custard to prevent a skin from forming.

In a small nonreactive saucepan (not nonstick), stir the sugar with ¼ cup water. Bring the mixture to a boil over medium heat, using a pastry brush dipped into cold water to brush any sugar crystals from the sides of the pan. Boil for 2 minutes, then remove from the heat and stir in the gelatin until it dissolves completely, at least 1 minute.

While the sugar is boiling, using a standing mixer fitted with the whisk attachment, beat the egg whites on high speed until they turn thick and foamy.

With the mixer running, pour the hot sugar syrup into the egg whites in a slow, steady stream, aiming it between the edge of the bowl and the beater. Continue beating for 5 minutes longer, or until the bottom of the bowl feels slightly warm to the touch. Add the vanilla and beat for 1 minute longer.

Without delay, transfer the topping to a piping bag fitted with a standard round tip. (Alternatively, use a resealable plastic bag: fill, press out the air, seal, and snip off one corner.) Pipe the topping onto the tarts in a spiral, starting at an outer edge and working your way toward the center. (If using store-bought topping, which does not pipe well, spoon it onto the tarts and toast it just before serving.)

To finish: Wave a kitchen torch over each tart to toast the topping. (Alternatively, broil the tarts on a baking sheet in the upper third of the oven for 30 to 45 seconds, watching carefully and removing them as soon as the topping browns.)

To serve: Cut each tart in half, and serve immediately.

Refrigerate leftover tarts made with the homemade topping, covered with plastic film, for up to 2 days after toasting.

# Deconstructed Key Lime Pie

PER SERVING: 250 CALORIES, 1.5 GRAMS FAT

## lime custard

1½ teaspoons (packed) finely grated lime zest (from about 1½ limes)

⅔ cup fresh lime juice (from about 6 limes)

⅓ cup Key lime juice, bottled or fresh (from about 10 Key limes)

One 14-ounce can fat-free sweetened condensed milk

2 tablespoons plus ½ teaspoon light coconut milk

4 egg whites from large eggs

2 large eggs

⅛ teaspoon salt

**MAKE AHEAD!**

The baked custards can be refrigerated, tightly wrapped, up to 3 days in advance, or frozen up to 1 week in advance. Thaw frozen custards overnight in the refrigerator.

I've given the traditional Key lime pie a contemporary makeover by baking the custard in ramekins or custard cups and serving them with a graham cracker and toasted marshmallow topping. Key limes are smaller and have a more intense flavor than the common (Persian) lime. I like the balance of the two combined. A bit of coconut milk in the custard adds flavor without much fat; use the rest of the can in the Piña Colada Popsicles (page 125).

To make the custard: Preheat the oven to 325°F with a rack in the center position.

In a medium bowl, combine the lime zest and both lime juices. Whisk in the condensed milk, coconut milk, egg whites, whole eggs, and salt.

Divide the custard mixture evenly among eight 3- to 4-ounce ramekins or oven-safe dessert cups. Set the ramekins into a deep baking dish that is large enough to hold them all. Fill a kettle with hot water. Put the baking dish onto the oven rack and pour in the hot water until it comes halfway up the sides of the ramekins. Lay a single sheet of aluminum foil over the entire baking dish, wrapping the edges tightly around it to hold in the steam. Bake until the filling jiggles slightly when you shake a single ramekin, 20 to 30 minutes. (Take care when removing the foil to avoid a blast of scalding steam.)

Carefully remove the baking dish from the oven and remove the foil (again with care). Let the baking dish cool for about 30 minutes, until you can safely transfer the ramekins from the water bath to a wire rack. Refrigerate the ramekins, uncovered, until they are completely cold, about 2 hours. Then cover them with plastic film and refrigerate until serving.

*recipe continues*

## topping

1 teaspoon unflavored gelatin powder

½ cup sugar

1 teaspoon pure vanilla extract

2 egg whites from large eggs

8 reduced-fat honey graham crackers (about 2½-inch squares)

To make the topping: Put 2 tablespoons water into a small bowl and sprinkle the gelatin evenly over it. Set aside for 2 to 3 minutes to soften.

Stir the sugar with ¼ cup water in a small saucepan over medium-low heat until the sugar dissolves. Remove from the heat and whisk in the softened gelatin, scraping the bowl to make sure you have added it all. Stir for a full minute to fully dissolve the gelatin. Stir in the vanilla. Set aside.

Using a standing mixer fitted with the whisk attachment, beat the egg whites on high speed until they are foamy. (Alternatively, use a hand-held electric mixer.) With the mixer running, add the syrup in a slow, steady stream, pouring it between the edge of the bowl and the whisk to avoid splattering. After all of the syrup is in, continue beating the whites until the bottom of the bowl feels cool to the touch, about 10 minutes. The mixture will look thick and shiny, like marshmallow creme.

Set out the ramekins and mound the topping over them, leaving some of the custard exposed around the edges. Use the back of a spoon to make decorative swirls. Refrigerate, uncovered, for up to 4 hours before serving.

To finish: Wave a kitchen torch slowly over the topping until it has the appearance of toasted marshmallow. (Alternatively, broil the ramekins on a baking sheet in the upper third of the oven for 30 to 45 seconds, watching carefully and removing them as soon as the topping is evenly toasted.)

To serve: For each dessert, break a graham cracker in half at the marking line. Crumble part of one piece to one side of the meringue, and plunge the other piece into the topping. Serve immediately.

# Nectarine-Blueberry Galette

SERVES 8

PER SERVING: 290 CALORIES, 7 GRAMS FAT
PER SERVING (SUGAR FREE): 240 CALORIES, 7 GRAMS FAT

Nonstick pan spray

Dough for 1 Cream Cheese Pie Crust (page 26)

½ cup sugar

1 vanilla bean

¼ teaspoon ground ginger

2 tablespoons all-purpose flour

4 medium nectarines, pitted and cut into ¼-inch-thick slices (about 5 cups)

1⅔ cups (about 12 ounces) blueberries

1 tablespoon fresh lemon juice

Luscious Whipped Topping (page 35) or store-bought whipped topping, for serving (optional)

I love the rustic look of a hand-formed galette. The edges bake to a golden brown and the fruit is exposed in the center, showing off its vibrant color. Galettes are also a lot less fussy and more forgiving than other pies and tarts, making them perfect for hesitant bakers.

Preheat the oven to 400°F with a rack in the center position. Coat a 10-inch ovenproof skillet with pan spray.

Roll the dough between two sheets of plastic film to form a 13-inch round that is about ⅛ inch thick. Unwrap the dough and transfer it to a baking sheet lined with parchment paper or waxed paper; cover it loosely with plastic film, and refrigerate it while you prepare the filling.

Put the sugar in a large bowl. Use a paring knife to slit the vanilla bean lengthwise and scrape the seeds into the sugar. Add the ginger. Use your fingers to rub the seeds and ginger into the sugar. Stir in the flour. Add the nectarine slices, blueberries, and lemon juice, stirring gently to evenly coat the fruit.

Press the chilled pastry into the bottom of the prepared skillet, leaving it loose along the sides. Pour the fruit mixture into the crust. Fold the sides of the crust over the fruit, pleating it as needed, to cover some of the fruit, with the fruit visible in the center.

*recipe continues*

Omit the sugar in the pie dough.

Substitute 5 tablespoons plus
¾ teaspoon (19 packets) of Truvía
for the sugar in the filling.

Bake the galette, rotating the pan once, for 40 to 45 minutes, until the crust is golden brown and the fruit is bubbling. If the exposed fruit begins to brown before the crust is baked through, loosely cover the fruit with aluminum foil.

Transfer the skillet to the stovetop or a wire rack and let it cool for 20 to 30 minutes.

*To serve:* Cut the galette into 8 wedges and serve each with a dollop of whipped topping, if desired.

Store any leftover galette, tightly wrapped, at room temperature for 1 day.

# Individual Walnut Cakes with Thyme Syrup and Orange

PER SERVING: 370 CALORIES, 13 GRAMS FAT

## walnut cakes

Nonstick pan spray

¾ cup all-purpose flour

½ cup whole wheat flour

¾ cup sugar

1 teaspoon baking soda

½ teaspoon ground cinnamon

⅛ teaspoon ground cloves

Pinch of salt

⅓ cup plus 1 tablespoon liquid egg substitute

⅓ cup plain nonfat Greek-style yogurt

¼ cup mild-flavored olive oil

1 tablespoon finely grated orange zest

2 tablespoons fresh orange juice

⅔ cup walnut halves, toasted

## thyme syrup

½ cup plus 2 tablespoons sugar

2 tablespoons honey

Six 2½-inch sprigs fresh thyme, plus 2 more for garnish

3 small oranges

In Greece, thyme grows wild all over the islands, its aroma filling the afternoon air. That captivating scent calls out for a dessert that captures the essence of the Greek islands. Orange trees are also common there, and oranges pair beautifully with thyme and walnuts. I love to showcase this Greek cake, known as *Karidopita,* at summer barbecues for friends and family, giving them a taste of paradise.

To make the cakes: Preheat the oven to 350°F with a rack in the center position. Coat eight 3-inch ring molds with pan spray and place them on a baking sheet lined with parchment paper or a silicone baking mat. (Alternatively, bake the cakes in muffin cups coated with pan spray.)

In a medium bowl, whisk together the all-purpose and whole wheat flours, sugar, baking soda, cinnamon, cloves, and salt. In a separate bowl, whisk together the egg substitute, yogurt, olive oil, orange zest, and orange juice.

Process the walnuts in a food processor for about 20 seconds, or until they are finely chopped. Add the flour mixture and process for 20 seconds. Add the egg mixture and pulse just until the dough clumps up around the blade.

Divide the batter evenly among the ring molds or muffin cups. Bake for 15 to 20 minutes, until a knife inserted into the center comes out clean.

recipe continues

Let the cakes cool in their molds on a wire rack for 5 minutes. Then remove from the molds or muffin cups, and let cool directly on the rack for 1 hour.

*To make the syrup:* Put the sugar into a small saucepan and add ½ cup plus 2 tablespoons water. Stir in the honey and the 6 thyme sprigs. Bring to a boil over medium heat, then continue to boil for 1 minute to fully dissolve the sugar. Pull out and discard the thyme sprigs.

Peel the oranges, trimming away any white pith. Working over a small bowl, use a paring knife to cut between the membranes and the flesh to release the orange segments into the bowl. Pour the warm syrup over the fruit.

*To serve:* Place the cakes on individual dessert plates, and divide the oranges evenly among them, spooning some of the syrup over each cake. Remove the leaves from the remaining thyme sprigs and sprinkle them on top of the oranges.

# Goat Cheesecake with Figs

SERVES 12

PER SERVING: 250 CALORIES, 11.5 GRAMS FAT

12 ounces (1½ cups) reduced-fat cream cheese (neufchâtel), preferably Kraft brand

½ cup sugar

5½ ounces chèvre, softened

⅓ cup low-fat buttermilk

¼ cup liquid egg substitute, or 1 large egg

2 egg whites from large eggs, at room temperature

1 Quick Graham Cracker Crust (page 25) in a 9-inch springform or other round cake pan

2 cups fresh Mission figs, rinsed and quartered

2 tablespoons finely chopped toasted pistachios

SERVING TIP

For a flavorful finish, drizzle lavender honey over the cheesecake just before serving.

I created this dessert when I was the pastry chef at LuLu restaurant in San Francisco. I was inspired by a goat cheese tart I had enjoyed on the Greek island of Santorini, where goat cheese and fresh figs are abundant. Chèvre is a mild fresh goat cheese that is naturally low in fat and calories; look for one with less than 5 grams of fat per ounce.

Preheat the oven to 325°F with a rack in the lower third of the oven.

Using an electric mixer, beat the cream cheese and sugar on medium speed for 2 to 3 minutes, until the mixture is smooth. (If using a standing mixer, use the paddle attachment.) Add the chèvre and beat for 2 to 3 minutes longer. Scrape down the sides of the bowl with a spatula. Add the buttermilk and egg substitute, and beat on low speed for 1 minute, then on medium for 2 minutes longer.

In a clean medium bowl, using clean beaters, beat the egg whites on high speed for 1 to 2 minutes, until medium peaks form, curling over slightly when you lift the beaters. Gently fold the whites into the cheesecake mixture just until combined.

Spread the cheesecake batter evenly over the crust. Bake for 20 minutes. Then tent a piece of aluminum foil over the pan and bake for 20 to 25 minutes longer, until the cheesecake is set and no longer jiggles.

Let the cheesecake cool at room temperature for 1 hour. Then refrigerate, loosely covered with plastic film, for at least another 2 hours or overnight.

To serve: If you used a springform pan, remove the outer ring and transfer the cake, on its base, to a serving platter. If you used a regular cake pan, cut the cake in the pan. Cut the cake into 12 wedges, and garnish each with the figs and pistachios.

# Lemon Tart with Brown Sugar Meringue

SERVES 12

PER SERVING: 310 CALORIES, 7.5 GRAMS FAT

## lemon filling

1⅓ cups granulated sugar

⅓ cup all-purpose flour

⅛ teaspoon salt

Finely grated zest of 1 lemon

1 cup fresh lemon juice (from about 6 large lemons), strained

¾ cup liquid egg substitute

2 large eggs

1 Graham Cracker Pie Crust (page 29) in a 10-inch tart pan with a removable bottom, baked (no need to cool)

MAKE AHEAD!

The filling can be made a day ahead and refrigerated, tightly covered. The finished tart can be refrigerated, tightly covered, for up to 4 hours before serving.

This lemony tart is buttery, sweet, and sour all at the same time. The brown sugar pairs wonderfully with the lemon. I was first introduced to brown sugar meringue by Gerry Moss, the former pastry chef at Tra Vigne restaurant in Napa Valley. Gerry insisted that hands were the best tools for applying meringue to a tart, creating irregular swirls that gave his tarts an edgy, contemporary look. So, go ahead and use your (impeccably clean) hands— it will be our little secret!

To make the filling: Preheat the oven to 350°F with a rack in the center position.

In a large bowl, whisk together the sugar, flour, and salt. Whisk in the lemon zest and lemon juice until the mixture is smooth. Whisk in the egg substitute, then the eggs.

Whisk the filling one more time and pour it in to fill the baked crust. (Bake any extra filling in a small oiled ramekin or custard cup.) Bake for 20 minutes, or until the filling no longer jiggles when you gently shake the pan.

Let the tart cool in the pan on a wire rack for 20 minutes. Then reach underneath the pan with your fingers and press up on the bottom of the pan, holding the sides with your thumbs, to find any sticky spots where curd may have seeped out between the crust and the pan. Use a paring knife to gently free the crust from the pan in these places. Remove the outer pan ring and transfer the tart, on its base, to a serving platter. Cover it loosely with plastic film and refrigerate for at least 5 hours.

## brown sugar meringue

⅔ cup (packed) dark brown sugar

½ cup egg whites (from 3 to
    4 large eggs)

To make the meringue: In a small nonreactive saucepan (not non-stick), stir the brown sugar with ¼ cup water. Bring the mixture to a boil over medium heat, and boil for 2 minutes.

While the sugar is boiling, using a standing mixer fitted with the whisk attachment, beat the egg whites on high speed until they turn thick and foamy. With the mixer running, pour the hot sugar syrup into the whites in a slow, steady stream, aiming it between the edge of the bowl and the whisk. Once all of the syrup has been added, continue beating for 5 minutes longer.

Immediately transfer the meringue to the top of the cold tart, and use a spatula or your clean hands to spread it over the top, creating dips, craters, and spikes.

To finish: Wave a kitchen torch over the tart to evenly brown the meringue. (Alternatively, broil the tart on a baking sheet in the upper third of the oven for 30 to 45 seconds, watching carefully and removing it as soon as the topping browns.)

To serve: Cut the tart into 12 wedges and serve immediately.

Refrigerate any leftover tart, tightly covered, for up to 2 days.

CHAPTER 6

# holiday favorites

*Holiday celebrations can present a special challenge* when you are trying to lose, or even just maintain, your weight. It's no fun to go to a Christmas party, or to a Fourth of July barbecue (aka swimsuit season), only to worry about counting calories.

This chapter is filled with recipes to help you make dessert a part of every holiday occasion. There are light solutions for Christmas and Thanksgiving, and sweet finales for Easter, Halloween, Mother's Day, and the Fourth of July.

This year, the holidays don't have to ruin your plans for staying trim, and you don't have to deprive yourself of indulging in something sweet as part of the festivities. From showstopping desserts like Chocolate-Peppermint Bûche de Noël to quick and easy ones like Sweet Potato Crème Brûlée, I have all of your holiday needs covered.

# Gingerbread Cutout Cookies

MAKES 25 TO 35 COOKIES

PER COOKIE: 50 CALORIES, 1 GRAM FAT

PER COOKIE (SUGAR FREE): 35 CALORIES, 1 GRAM FAT

## cookies

Nonstick pan spray (if not using baking mats or parchment)

1½ cups all-purpose flour

2 teaspoons ground ginger

1 teaspoon ground cinnamon

Scant ½ teaspoon ground cloves

¼ teaspoon baking soda

¼ teaspoon baking powder

¼ teaspoon freshly ground black pepper (ground fine)

⅛ teaspoon salt

1½ ounces (3 tablespoons) reduced-fat cream cheese (neufchâtel)

1½ tablespoons unsalted butter, softened

⅓ cup plus 1 tablespoon (packed) dark brown sugar

¼ cup liquid egg substitute, or 1 large egg

¼ cup plus 1 tablespoon unsulfured molasses

## royal icing

⅓ cup powdered sugar

1 tablespoon dried egg whites

Liquid food coloring (optional)

Every year, I make gingerbread cookies in festive shapes: snowflakes, gingerbread girls and boys, and frosted candy canes, to name a few. When the cookie cutters come out and the air becomes heavily scented with ginger and cloves, I know Christmas is right around the corner. The dried egg whites (also known as powdered egg whites) can be found in the baking aisle of many supermarkets and at gourmet food stores.

**To make the cookies:** Coat two baking sheets with pan spray, or line them with silicone baking mats or parchment paper.

In a bowl, whisk together the flour, ginger, cinnamon, cloves, baking soda, baking powder, pepper, and salt; set aside.

Using a standing mixer fitted with the paddle attachment, beat the cream cheese, butter, and brown sugar on medium speed for 4 minutes, or until the color lightens. (Alternatively, use a handheld electric mixer.) Scrape down the bowl. Add the egg substitute and molasses, beating until they are well combined. Add the flour mixture on low speed, just until it is incorporated.

Transfer the dough to a flat surface and roll it out between two pieces of plastic film until it is ⅛ inch thick. Peel off the top film and use cookie cutters to cut the dough into shapes. Reroll the dough scraps and cut out cookies up to two more times, to make 25 to 35 cookies. Transfer the cookies to the prepared pans, cover with plastic film, and freeze for 30 minutes or refrigerate for 2 hours.

recipe continues

Substitute ¼ cup plus 1 teaspoon (16 packets) of Truvía for the brown sugar in the cookies. Replace the molasses with 1¼ teaspoons instant espresso powder mixed with 1½ tablespoons water. Increase the ginger to 1 tablespoon, and add ¼ teaspoon ground star anise. The sugar-free cookies will puff slightly when baking; avoid using a patterned cookie cutter, as the detail will be lost.

For the icing, combine ¼ cup cornstarch, 1 tablespoon (4 packets) of Truvía, and 1 tablespoon dried egg whites in a clean coffee grinder or a food processor for 1 minute. Transfer the mixture to a small bowl and whisk in 2 tablespoons water. The icing color will be off-white but is lovely when colored. Brush or pipe the icing over the cookies as described.

About 20 minutes before baking, preheat the oven to 350°F with racks in the upper and lower thirds of the oven.

Bake the cookies for 25 minutes, or until the tops no longer appear moist and shiny. Halfway through the baking time, rotate the baking sheets from top to bottom and front to back. When the cookies are done, set the sheets on wire racks and leave them for at least 30 minutes, until the cookies are cool to the touch.

To make the icing: Sift the powdered sugar and dried egg whites through a fine-mesh strainer into a small bowl. Whisk in 2 teaspoons water until the mixture is well blended. If you are coloring the icing, divide the icing into small bowls, one for each color, and stir in a drop or two of coloring to create the desired color.

Brush the icing onto the cookies with a pastry brush. (Alternatively, use small piping bags or resealable plastic bags—one for each color, each fitted with a small round tip—to pipe decorative patterns onto the cookies.) Let the icing set for 20 minutes before serving.

Store any leftover cookies at room temperature in an airtight container, layered between sheets of waxed paper, for up to 3 weeks.

# Holiday Pumpkin Pie

One 15-ounce can pumpkin puree

One 12-ounce can low-fat (1%) evaporated milk

½ cup (packed) dark brown sugar

¼ cup granulated sugar

2 egg whites from large eggs, or ⅓ cup liquid egg whites

1 large egg

1 teaspoon ground cinnamon

⅛ teaspoon ground nutmeg

⅛ to ½ teaspoon ground ginger, to taste

Scant ½ teaspoon salt

½ vanilla bean, or ½ teaspoon pure vanilla extract

3 tablespoons unsulfured molasses (optional)

¼ teaspoon ground cloves (optional)

1 Cream Cheese Pie Crust (page 26), baked blind in a 9 × 2-inch pie pan or a 10-inch pie or tart pan, cooled

Luscious Whipped Topping (page 35) or store-bought whipped topping, for serving (optional)

For me, pumpkin pie is a Thanksgiving Day "must." This one is perfect for winding up the holiday on a welcomed lighter note. I like my pumpkin pie mildly spiced, but if you prefer it spicier, the optional molasses and cloves will get you there. The pie is equally good at room temperature or refrigerated.

Preheat the oven to 350°F with a rack in the center position.

In a medium bowl, whisk together the pumpkin and evaporated milk until smooth. Add the brown sugar, granulated sugar, egg whites, whole egg, cinnamon, nutmeg, ginger, and salt. Use a paring knife to slit the vanilla bean lengthwise and scrape the seeds into the bowl, or stir in the vanilla extract. Whisk in the molasses and cloves, if desired.

Pour the filling into the cooled crust and bake for 40 to 45 minutes, until the pie puffs up in the center and no longer jiggles when you shake it gently.

Transfer the pie to a wire rack to cool completely, about 1 hour.

To serve: Cut the pie into 12 wedges and top with whipped topping, if desired.

Refrigerate any leftover pie, tightly covered, for 2 to 3 days.

# Bacon Toffee for the Contemporary Cookie Tin

MAKES APPROXIMATELY 45 CANDIES

PER CANDY: 50 CALORIES, 2 GRAMS FAT

Four ¼-inch-thick slices smoked bacon, preferably applewood smoked

2½ teaspoons smoked paprika

½ teaspoon salt

Scant ½ teaspoon baking soda

1¼ cups sugar

2½ tablespoons light corn syrup

¼ cup (½ stick) unsalted butter, softened

½ cup milk chocolate chips

1 teaspoon smoked coarse sea salt, for garnish

To some, bacon may sound like an odd addition to a dessert. But as anyone who has dipped that breakfast staple into maple syrup can attest, its salty-smoky flavor pairs perfectly with something sweet. Smoked paprika allows you to use less bacon and still have plenty of flavor. Baking soda is another surprise ingredient—it replaces some of the butter, balancing the sweetness and enhancing the toffee's crisp, buttery texture. (See photo on page 204.)

Line a baking sheet with a silicone baking mat or parchment paper.

Heat a skillet over medium-high heat. Add the bacon and cook for about 2 minutes on each side, until the edges are crisp and brown. Reduce the heat to medium and continue to cook until the bacon is crisp all over. Blot the bacon with a paper towel and transfer it to the prepared baking sheet. Let the bacon cool for 5 minutes, then transfer it to a cutting board and finely chop it. Put the chopped bacon into a small bowl and sprinkle it with the smoked paprika, salt, and baking soda, tossing to coat. Set aside the bacon and the lined baking sheet.

In a small nonreactive saucepan (stainless steel or copper works best; avoid nonstick), stir together the sugar, corn syrup, and ⅓ cup water to completely moisten the sugar. Bring the mixture to a boil over medium heat, using a pastry brush dipped into cold water to brush any sugar crystals from the sides of the pan. After the sugar dissolves and the

MY TRICK
FOR QUICK
CLEANUP

Fill the saucepan with water and boil it for 20 minutes to remove the hardened sugar.

mixture is clear and bubbling, raise the heat to medium-high. Add the butter, a spoonful at a time, without stirring, allowing it to melt between additions. Once the mixture begins to turn light golden, stir it with a heatproof spatula as needed to cook evenly. When the mixture turns a deep golden color, remove the pan from the heat, and working carefully (the caramel will be very hot!), vigorously stir in the bacon-paprika mixture.

Immediately pour the toffee onto the prepared baking sheet and spread it into a thin layer, covering the entire sheet. Let the toffee cool for 15 minutes, or until it is set. Then invert the pan over a flat surface to release the toffee from the baking mat, and break it into about 45 pieces.

Melt the chocolate chips in the top of a double boiler until you can stir them smooth. (Alternatively, use a microwave oven.) Use a butter knife to spread a thin layer of chocolate onto one flat side of the toffee pieces, and sprinkle with the smoked salt. Let the chocolate firm up for 20 minutes before serving.

Refrigerate any leftover toffee in an airtight container for up to 1 week.

# Coconut-Lime Truffles

MAKES 35 TRUFFLES

PER TRUFFLE: 60 CALORIES, 4 GRAMS FAT

12 ounces (2½ cups) white chocolate chips

¼ cup 1% milk

¼ cup light coconut milk

1 tablespoon Malibu rum, or 2½ teaspoons dark rum plus ½ teaspoon imitation coconut extract

Finely grated zest of 1 lime

1 tablespoon fresh lime juice

¼ cup plus 2 tablespoons unsweetened shredded coconut, plus more (optional) for coating the truffles

Chocolate truffles are as simple to make as they are elegant. They are lovely served on platters at holiday parties or packaged as gifts. The combination of white chocolate and lime makes this truffle taste like a bite of Key lime pie. I've replaced the cream normally found in truffles with a blend of reduced-fat milks, and some of the chocolate with shredded coconut, so you can indulge without worrying about fitting into your favorite holiday outfit. (See photo on page 204.)

Line two baking sheets with waxed paper or plastic film.

Melt 1 cup plus 1 tablespoon of the white chocolate chips with the 1% milk in the top of a double boiler, or in a microwave oven, until you can stir the mixture smooth. Stir in the coconut milk, rum, lime zest, lime juice, and shredded coconut until thoroughly combined. Freeze the mixture, loosely covered with plastic film, for 1 to 2 hours, until firm and scoopable, or refrigerate it overnight.

Scoop the truffle mixture in heaping teaspoons onto one of the prepared baking sheets to make 35 truffles. Roll each truffle between the palms of your hands to make a ball. Freeze the truffles, loosely covered with plastic film, for 1 hour.

Melt the remaining chocolate chips in the top of a double boiler, or in a microwave oven, until you can stir them smooth.

MAKE
AHEAD!

The undipped truffles, rolled into balls, can be frozen in an airtight container, the layers separated with waxed paper, for up to 1 month. Coat in chocolate before serving.

To keep them very cold, remove just 6 of the truffles from the freezer at a time. One at a time, drop a truffle into the melted chocolate, spoon a little chocolate over the top to completely cover the surface, and then immediately lift it out with a fork, allowing any residual chocolate to drip back into the bowl. Transfer the truffle to the second prepared baking sheet. Sprinkle additional coconut over the dipped truffle, if desired. Repeat to coat the remaining truffles. (If the chocolate becomes too thick to dip, reheat it briefly before continuing.) Refrigerate the dipped truffles, uncovered, for 30 minutes, or until the chocolate shell is hard.

Pack any leftover truffles in an airtight container, separating the layers with waxed paper, and refrigerate for up to 2 weeks.

Top to bottom: Orange-Chile Chocolate
Bark (opposite), Coconut-Lime Truffles
(page 202), and Bacon Toffee for the
Contemporary Cookie Tin (page 200).

Sweet & Skinny

# Orange-Chile Chocolate Bark

MAKES 12 CANDIES

PER CANDY: 60 CALORIES, 3.5 GRAMS FAT

1 cup (5 ounces) chopped good-quality dark chocolate

½ cup crisped rice cereal

1½ teaspoons finely grated orange zest

½ teaspoon cayenne pepper

Chocolate bark makes a fun and easy holiday gift. Crispy rice cereal gives it the feel of a gourmet crunch bar, but it has another purpose: it cuts the chocolate (including its fat and calories) by one-third! A little surge of heat from the cayenne is a wonderful surprise that sneaks up on you as the chocolate dissolves on your tongue.

TEMPERING
CHOCOLATE

Melting part of the chocolate and then stirring in the rest at the end is a quick trick for tempering, the technique that gives chocolate its snap and shine, and prevents white streaks from forming on the chocolate over time. Pastry chef Cheryl Lew taught me another trick to eliminate those bothersome (though harmless) white streaks when they do form: lightly coat the streaky chocolate with nonstick pan spray to return its shine!

Line a baking sheet with waxed paper or a silicone baking mat.

Melt two-thirds of the chocolate in the top of a double boiler until you can stir it smooth. (Alternatively, use a microwave oven.) Stir in the remaining third of the chocolate until it is completely melted.

Put the cereal into a medium bowl and toss with the orange zest and cayenne to evenly distribute them. Stir the mixture into the melted chocolate, then spread it onto the prepared baking sheet in a thin, even layer, about 6 × 9 inches. Refrigerate the bark for 15 minutes, or until it is firm.

To serve: Break the bark into 12 pieces.

Refrigerate any leftover bark in an airtight container, separating the layers with waxed paper, for up to 2 weeks.

# Tiramisù Layer Cake

## coffee syrup

¼ cup strong brewed coffee, at room temperature

¼ cup plus 1 tablespoon Kahlúa

## mousse

½ cup fat-free evaporated milk

1 teaspoon unflavored gelatin powder

10 ounces (1¼ cups) reduced-fat cream cheese (neufchâtel), preferably Kraft brand

½ cup plus 1 tablespoon sugar

½ cup reduced-fat ricotta cheese

Chocolate sponge cake from Chocolate-Peppermint Bûche de Noël (page 211), cooled

¼ cup cocoa nibs

2 tablespoons unsweetened natural or Dutch-processed cocoa powder

Birthdays are not exactly a holiday, but since they are a cause for celebration, I wanted to include a birthday cake in this holiday chapter. This sophisticated, grown-up cake combines fluffy ricotta cheese with cocoa, coffee, and Kahlúa, making it perfect for coffee lovers. Now there's no reason to go without cake on your birthday!

To make the syrup: Stir together the coffee and Kahlúa in a small bowl. Set aside.

To make the mousse: Pour ¼ cup of the evaporated milk into a small saucepan. Whisk in the gelatin and let it soften for 3 minutes. Then cook over medium heat, stirring, until the milk is hot but not boiling and the gelatin has dissolved completely, about 3 minutes.

Transfer the hot milk to a medium bowl and stir in the remaining ¼ cup evaporated milk. Freeze just until the edges of the milk begin to set, about 10 minutes.

While the milk is chilling, use an electric mixer to beat the cream cheese and sugar on medium speed for 1 to 2 minutes, until creamy. (If using a standing mixer, use the paddle attachment.) Add the ricotta and beat for 1 minute longer. Set aside.

Use an electric mixer to beat the chilled milk mixture on high speed for 4 to 5 minutes, until it resembles whipped cream. Mix the cream cheese mixture into the whipped milk.

*To assemble:* Run a small paring knife around the perimeter of the chocolate sponge cake. Lay out a sheet of waxed paper slightly larger than the cake pan, and invert the pan over the waxed paper. Remove the pan and parchment paper.

Using an 8-inch springform pan as a guide, cut two rounds from the cake. Reserve the remaining cake scraps. Fit one cake round into the bottom of the springform pan. Use a pastry brush to paint the cake with one-third of the coffee syrup. Spread one-third of the mousse over the cake. Sprinkle with one-third of the cocoa nibs.

Cut and fit the reserved cake scraps over the filling. Repeat the brushing and filling, using half of the remaining syrup, mousse, and cocoa nibs. Make a final layer using the second cake round and all of the remaining syrup and mousse. (Reserve the remaining cocoa nibs for garnish.) Cover the pan tightly with plastic film and refrigerate for at least 1 hour, until cold.

Run a dishcloth under warm water and wring it out. Wrap the warm cloth around the springform pan for 1 minute to loosen the cake. Then remove the pan sides and transfer the cake, on its base, to a serving plate. Sift the cocoa powder over the top and sprinkle with the reserved cocoa nibs.

*To serve:* Cut the cake into 16 wedges, dipping the blade of a sharp knife into hot water and wiping it dry between cuts.

# Independence Day Float

PER SERVING: 160 CALORIES, 0 GRAMS FAT

## syrup

Nine ¼-inch-thick slices peeled
fresh ginger

1 cup sugar

½ pint (1 cup) ripe blackberries

2½ tablespoons elderflower
liqueur, such as St-Germain

## sorbet

1½ cups ripe strawberries, hulled

Scant ¼ cup agave nectar

6 cups club soda, chilled

MAKE
AHEAD!

The blackberry-elderflower syrup
can be made up to 10 days in
advance and refrigerated in a
tightly covered container. The sorbet can be made up to 5 days in
advance and frozen in an airtight
container.

This adult version of an ice cream float is fragrant with blackberries, elderflower, and strawberries. The colors are striking as they slowly shift from deep purple to light blue. It's the perfect addition to a memorable Fourth of July. A simple puree of ripe strawberries sweetened with a bit of agave nectar freezes into a sorbet texture without ever seeing the inside of an ice cream machine.

To make the syrup: Put the ginger and sugar into a small saucepan and add 1 cup water. Bring the mixture to a boil over medium heat, then boil for 10 minutes, until it is somewhat thickened.

Put the blackberries in a medium bowl and mash them with a fork. Pour the hot syrup over the berries and let steep for 30 minutes. Strain through a fine-mesh strainer into a small bowl. Stir in the liqueur. Refrigerate if not using immediately.

To make the sorbet: Process the strawberries and agave nectar in a blender until the mixture is smooth. Transfer to a covered container and freeze for 2 hours, until firm.

To serve: Use a small scoop to divide the sorbet among six tall glasses. Add 1 cup of chilled club soda to each. Pour 3 to 4 tablespoons of the syrup into each glass, depending on your preferred sweetness. Do not stir; instead, allow the syrup to swirl and mix in on its own, creating a lovely visual effect. Serve with a straw and an iced tea spoon.

# Chocolate-Peppermint Bûche de Noël

PER SERVING: 170 CALORIES, 8 GRAMS FAT

## chocolate sponge cake

Nonstick pan spray

½ cup all-purpose flour

¼ cup unsweetened Dutch-
  processed cocoa powder

⅛ teaspoon salt

2 large eggs

5 egg whites from large eggs

⅔ cup plus ¼ cup granulated
  sugar

MAKE AHEAD!

This cake has many options for advance preparation. The sponge cake can be made up to 1 day ahead and stored, covered with plastic film, at room temperature. The frosting can be refrigerated, tightly covered, up to 2 days in advance. The bark can be refrigerated, in an airtight container layered between sheets of waxed paper, up to 2 days ahead. The cake can be filled and rolled a day ahead, then frosted and finished the following day. Finally, the finished *bûche* can be refrigerated, covered, up to 2 days in advance.

Bûche de Noël is one of my favorite desserts to serve on Christmas Day. It makes an impressive centerpiece for the dinner table, and though there are many steps, it is surprisingly easy to prepare. Making all or some of the parts in advance can help keep the holiday a little less hectic.

*To make the sponge cake:* Preheat the oven to 400°F with a rack in the upper third of the oven. Coat a 17 × 12-inch rimmed baking sheet with pan spray and line the bottom with parchment paper.

In a small bowl, stir together the flour, cocoa powder, and salt.

Using a standing mixer fitted with the whisk attachment, beat the eggs and 1 egg white on high speed until they are foamy. Gradually add the ⅔ cup sugar, a few teaspoons at a time, and continue beating until the eggs are thick and tripled in volume, about 5 minutes total. Add the flour mixture on low speed, then increase to medium for 10 to 15 seconds. (Alternatively, use a handheld electric mixer.)

In a clean bowl, using clean beaters, beat the remaining 4 egg whites on high speed until they are foamy. Gradually add the remaining ¼ cup sugar, a few teaspoons at a time. Beat for about 4 minutes longer, until medium peaks form, curling over like soft-serve ice cream when you lift the beaters. Use a large spatula to gently fold the whites into the cake batter just until no visible white streaks remain.

Spread the batter evenly into the prepared baking sheet. Bake just until the cake feels soft and springy in the center when you press it lightly with your fingers, 8 to 10 minutes. Transfer the sheet to a wire rack to cool completely, about 30 minutes.

recipe continues

## frosting

8 ounces (1⅓ cups) semisweet
    chocolate chips

⅔ cup low-fat sour cream, at room
    temperature

½ teaspoon pure peppermint
    extract

Powdered sugar, for rolling and
    decorating

## bark

⅓ cup semisweet chocolate chips

Candy canes or pine branches, for
    decorating (optional)

**To make the frosting:** Melt the chocolate chips in the top of a double boiler, or in a microwave oven, until you can stir them smooth. Whisk in the sour cream until it is completely blended. Stir in the peppermint extract. Let the frosting cool completely.

**To fill and roll the cake:** Run a paring knife around the perimeter of the baking sheet to loosen the cake. Lay out a large sheet of waxed paper on a flat surface and dust it lightly with powdered sugar. Invert the sheet over the waxed paper, then remove the sheet and carefully peel the parchment paper off the cake. Pour and spread one-third of the frosting over the cake. (Reserve the remaining frosting.)

Set the cake with a long side facing you. Using the waxed paper as an aid, roll the cake away from you into a long, tight log. Twist the ends of the waxed paper tightly to hold the cake snugly. Transfer the cake roll to a baking sheet and refrigerate for 1 hour.

**To make the bark:** Melt the chocolate chips in the top of a double boiler, or in a microwave oven, until you can stir them smooth. Lay a sheet of waxed paper on a flat surface and spread the melted chocolate over it in a thin, even layer. Refrigerate until the bark is firm and no longer shiny, about 30 minutes.

Turn the waxed paper chocolate-side-down on a flat surface, and carefully peel away the paper. Break the chocolate into long strips resembling wood bark.

*To finish:* Cut a 5-inch-long piece from one end of the cake roll on the diagonal, to use as a branch. Position the long cake log on a serving tray and use two-thirds of the remaining frosting to cover the top and sides of the roll. Position the small cake branch with a cut side against the log near one end to make a Y-shaped branch. Frost the small branch. Arrange the chocolate bark on the cake, anchoring it in the frosting. Sift powdered sugar over the top and decorate with candy canes or pine branches, if desired.

*To serve:* Use a large chef's knife to cut the cake into 16 pieces, dipping the blade into hot water and wiping it dry between cuts.

# Pear and Chocolate Gingerbread Upside-Down Cake

SERVES 16

PER SERVING: 180 CALORIES, 6 GRAMS FAT

Nonstick pan spray

### topping

⅓ cup (packed) dark brown sugar

⅓ cup granulated sugar

2 ripe Bartlett or Anjou pears, peeled, cored, and cut into ½-inch-thick slices

### cake

1 cup all-purpose flour

½ cup unsweetened Dutch-processed cocoa powder

¼ teaspoon ground ginger

¼ teaspoon ground cinnamon

¼ teaspoon ground cloves

⅛ teaspoon salt

⅔ cup plain nonfat Greek-style yogurt

½ cup (packed) dark brown sugar

¼ cup unsulfured molasses

⅓ cup canola oil

¼ cup liquid egg substitute

3 tablespoons freshly grated ginger

2 teaspoons instant espresso powder plus ⅓ cup boiling water, or ⅓ cup hot strong coffee

1 teaspoon baking soda

Luscious Whipped Topping (page 35) or store-bought whipped topping, for garnish (optional)

My first introduction to chocolate and ginger was as a child on Saint Nicholas Day—the day of gift-giving celebrated in many European countries and, to my delight, in our home. That year I found a beautifully wrapped dark chocolate and ginger candy bar tucked into my goodie bag. The sweet, fruity, mildly spiced combination was utterly wonderful. This luscious holiday cake, topped with caramelized pears, brings back that happy memory.

Preheat the oven to 350°F with a rack in the center position. Generously coat a 9-inch square cake pan with pan spray.

To make the topping: In a small bowl, mix together the brown and granulated sugars. Sprinkle the mixture evenly over the bottom of the prepared pan. Arrange the pears in the pan, spacing them evenly.

To make the cake: In a medium bowl, whisk together the flour, cocoa powder, ground ginger, cinnamon, cloves, and salt.

In a large bowl, whisk together the yogurt, brown sugar, molasses, oil, egg substitute, and grated ginger. Add the flour mixture, stirring just until it is incorporated.

In a small bowl, mix the espresso powder with the boiling water. Whisk in the baking soda. (If using hot brewed coffee, whisk the baking soda into the coffee.) Mix the coffee mixture into the batter.

recipe continues

MAKE AHEAD!

Prepare the batter up to 1 day in advance and refrigerate in a covered container. Spread the batter over the pears in the pan just before baking.

Spread the cake batter evenly over the pears, taking care not to disturb their position. The bottom of the pan and the pears should be completely covered with the batter.

Bake for 35 minutes, or until a knife inserted into the center comes out clean.

Let the cake cool in the pan on a wire rack for 5 minutes. Then invert a serving plate over the pan, carefully grip the pan and plate together with oven mitts, and flip them over to release the cake onto the plate. Lift off the cake pan and let the cake cool for at least 2 hours before serving.

*To serve:* Cut the cake into 4 equal pieces one way, then 4 the other, to make 16 squares. Serve with whipped topping, if desired.

Store any leftover cake, tightly wrapped, at room temperature for up to 2 days.

# Sugar & Spice
# White Chocolate Cupcakes

MAKES 12 CUPCAKES

PER CUPCAKE: 210 CALORIES, 8 GRAMS FAT

## cupcakes

1 cup cake flour

2 teaspoons ground cinnamon

1 teaspoon baking powder

⅛ teaspoon freshly grated nutmeg

Pinch of salt

⅓ cup pureed cooked carrots

¼ cup Browned Butter (page 24), melted

3 tablespoons nonfat milk

1 teaspoon pure vanilla extract

2 large eggs

1 egg white from a large egg

½ cup plus 1 tablespoon granulated sugar

MAKE AHEAD!

The frosting can be refrigerated, tightly covered, up to 5 days in advance.

These cupcakes are a fun and festive holiday dessert. Pureed carrots give them a warm color and bring out the cinnamon's toasty notes (canned pumpkin will also work). For a sophisticated presentation, the cupcakes are topped with cinnamon sticks and star anise as a hint to what awaits.

Preheat the oven to 350°F with a rack in the center position. Line 12 muffin cups with paper liners.

To make the cupcakes: Sift the flour, cinnamon, baking powder, nutmeg, and salt into a small bowl. Stir together the carrots, butter, milk, and vanilla in another small bowl. Set both bowls aside.

Using a standing mixer fitted with the whisk attachment, beat the eggs and egg white on high speed until they are foamy. (Alternatively, use a handheld electric mixer.) With the mixer running, gradually add the sugar, a few teaspoons at a time. Continue to mix for 8 minutes longer.

Use a large spatula to gently fold half of the flour mixture into the eggs. Fold in all of the carrot mixture, and then the remaining flour, folding gently just until it is incorporated. Scoop the batter into the lined muffin cups.

Bake the cupcakes for 13 to 15 minutes, until a wooden skewer inserted into the center comes out clean. Transfer the pan to a wire rack and let the cupcakes cool completely, about 2 hours.

recipe continues

## frosting

⅓ cup (packed) dark brown sugar

3 ounces (6 tablespoons) reduced-fat cream cheese (neufchâtel)

½ teaspoon ground cinnamon

Pinch of ground or freshly grated star anise

Pinch of salt

3 ounces white chocolate, melted

½ teaspoon pure vanilla extract

12 short cinnamon sticks, for garnish (optional)

12 star anise pods, for garnish (optional)

**To make the frosting:** Using an electric mixer, beat the brown sugar, cream cheese, cinnamon, anise, and salt on medium speed for 2 to 3 minutes, until the mixture is smooth. (If using a standing mixer, use the paddle attachment.) Add the melted chocolate and the vanilla; beat for 1 minute longer.

**To finish:** Spread a heaping tablespoon of frosting over each cupcake using a small spatula or a butter knife. While the frosting is still soft, press a cinnamon stick and a star anise pod, if using, into the top of each cupcake.

Store any leftover cupcakes, loosely wrapped with plastic film, at room temperature for up to 2 days.

EASY
CARROT
PUREE

A jar of Gerber baby carrots is my secret source of carrot puree for this recipe. If you prefer to make your own, boil 2 medium carrots until they are very soft and then blend them with just enough of the cooking liquid to make a smooth puree. Measure ⅓ cup for the recipe.

# Sweet Potato Crème Brûlée

1 sweet potato, baked or microwaved until soft

½ vanilla bean

1⅛ cups 2% milk

½ cup plus 2 tablespoons half-and-half

Scant ¼ cup liquid egg substitute

2½ tablespoons granulated sugar

2½ tablespoons (packed) dark brown sugar

⅛ teaspoon freshly grated nutmeg

⅛ teaspoon ground ginger

6 tablespoons granulated sugar

This twist on a classic is a nice alternative to pumpkin pie for Thanksgiving—but that doesn't mean you should wait for a special occasion to make it! Crème brûlée fans will delight in this creamy yet slender version of a notoriously rich dessert. Use a sweet potato variety with dark skin and moist orange flesh.

Preheat the oven to 325°F with a rack in the center position. Arrange six crème brûlée ramekins (or other shallow ramekins) in two 13 × 9-inch baking pans. Set aside.

Scoop out ¾ cup of the flesh from the sweet potato and place it in a blender. Use a paring knife to slit the vanilla bean lengthwise and scrape the seeds into the blender. Add the milk, half-and-half, egg substitute, granulated sugar, brown sugar, nutmeg, and ginger. Blend for 30 seconds, until smooth. Strain through a fine-mesh strainer into a glass measure or a bowl with a pouring spout. Divide the mixture evenly among the ramekins.

Cover the baking pans with aluminum foil, sealing the foil tightly on three sides and leaving it lifted on the fourth side. Place the pans on the oven rack with the open edges closest to you, and pour warm water into the pans to reach halfway up the sides of the ramekins. Seal the open sides.

Bake the custards for 40 to 45 minutes, until the custard is just slightly jiggly in the center when you gently shake a ramekin. (Be careful when peeling back the foil, to avoid the burst of hot steam.)

MAKE
AHEAD!

Refrigerate the custards for up to 1 day before finishing with the sugar topping and serving.

Transfer the baking pans to a flat surface, taking care not to slosh water into the ramekins. Remove the foil and let cool for 30 minutes, until you can comfortably transfer the ramekins from the water bath to a rimmed baking sheet. Cover the ramekins lightly with plastic film and refrigerate for at least 4 hours, until cold.

To finish: Sprinkle 1 tablespoon of the granulated sugar evenly over each custard. Wave a kitchen torch over each ramekin until the sugar is melted and amber all over. (Alternatively, place the ramekins on a baking sheet and broil in the upper third of the oven for 1 to 2 minutes, watching carefully and removing them as soon as the sugar melts and turns amber.) Let cool for several minutes, just until the sugar hardens, then serve.

# Meyer Lemon Easter Cupcakes

## cupcakes

1 cup cake flour

1 teaspoon baking powder

¼ teaspoon salt

¼ cup mild-flavored olive oil

Scant 1 tablespoon grated Meyer lemon zest (from 1 to 2 lemons)

3 tablespoons fresh Meyer lemon juice

2 tablespoons 2% milk

2 large eggs

1 egg white from a large egg

½ cup granulated sugar

MAKE AHEAD!

The frosting can be refrigerated, tightly covered, up to 4 days in advance.

These cupcakes are just right for Easter, with their pale yellow color and a toasted coconut topping that's perfect for turning the tops into dainty birds' nests. A cross between a traditional lemon and a mandarin orange, the Meyer lemon has deep yellow skin, an intoxicating fragrance, and an alluring sweet-tart flavor. If Meyer lemons aren't available, substitute 2 teaspoons lemon zest and 1 teaspoon orange zest for the zest in the cupcakes, and the same for the zest in the frosting. For the juice in the cupcakes, substitute 2 tablespoons lemon juice plus 1 tablespoon orange juice.

Preheat the oven to 350°F with a rack in the center position. Line 12 muffin cups with paper liners.

To make the cupcakes: Sift the flour, baking powder, and salt into a small bowl. In another small bowl, whisk together the olive oil, lemon zest and juice, and milk. Set the bowls aside.

Using a standing mixer fitted with the whisk attachment, beat the eggs and egg white on high speed until they are foamy. (Alternatively, use a handheld electric mixer.) Gradually add the sugar, a few teaspoons at a time, and continue to beat for 5 minutes longer, until the mixture is thick and tripled in volume.

Sift half of the flour mixture over the eggs, and gently fold it in with a spatula. Mix in the olive oil mixture. Sift the remaining flour mixture over the batter and fold just until it is incorporated. Divide the batter evenly among the lined muffin cups.

Bake the cupcakes for 13 to 15 minutes, until a wooden skewer inserted into the center of one comes out clean. Transfer the pan to a wire rack and let the muffins cool, about 2 hours.

## frosting

¾ cup powdered sugar

4 ounces (½ cup) reduced-fat cream cheese (neufchâtel)

Finely grated zest of 1 Meyer lemon

2 ounces white chocolate, melted

½ cup toasted sweetened flake coconut, for garnish

36 jelly beans, for garnish

To make the frosting: Using an electric mixer, beat the powdered sugar, cream cheese, and lemon zest on medium speed until the mixture is smooth. (If using a standing mixer, use the paddle attachment.) Add the melted chocolate and beat for 1 minute longer.

To finish: Spread a heaping tablespoon of frosting over each cupcake, using a small spatula or a butter knife. Sprinkle the coconut around the outer edge and press 3 jelly beans into the center of each frosted cupcake. Let the frosting set, uncovered, at room temperature for about 1 hour.

Store any leftover cupcakes, loosely wrapped with plastic film, at room temperature for up to 2 days.

# Baked Apples with Maple-Gingersnap Stuffing

SERVES 4

PER SERVING: 260 CALORIES, 7 GRAMS FAT

Nonstick pan spray

8 crisp gingersnap cookies, such as Nabisco Ginger Snaps

3 tablespoons raisins, coarsely chopped

2 tablespoons pecans, coarsely chopped

1 tablespoon unsalted butter, melted

½ teaspoon ground cinnamon

¼ teaspoon ground ginger

4 small Pink Lady apples

¼ cup pure maple syrup

2 tablespoons apple juice

Vanilla Ice Cream (page 37) or Dreyer's Slow Churned Vanilla Ice Cream, for serving (optional)

These apples are the perfect holiday dessert when you are pressed for time. The maple syrup, cinnamon, and gingersnaps fill the air with a festive fragrance as they bake. The recipe highlights one of the loveliest winter fruits, the Pink Lady apple—one of the last apples of the season. Choose apples that stand up straight on their base.

Preheat the oven to 350°F with a rack in the center position. Coat a 9-inch square baking pan with pan spray.

Put the cookies into a resealable plastic bag, close, and crush using a mallet until the cookies are in crumbs. Set aside 2 tablespoons and put the rest into a bowl. Stir in the raisins, pecans, butter, cinnamon, and ginger.

Cut a ¼-inch slice from the top of each apple. Use a small spoon or a paring knife to scoop out the cores, including a bit of the flesh, to create an opening that is about 2 inches deep and 1½ inches wide. Pack the gingersnap stuffing into the apples, and place them in the prepared baking pan.

In a small bowl, stir together the maple syrup and apple juice. Spoon the mixture over the filling in the apples, using about 1 tablespoon for each and reserving the last 2 tablespoons.

Bake the apples for 20 minutes. Spoon the remaining syrup over the apples, sprinkle them with the reserved 2 tablespoons crushed gingersnaps, and bake for 20 minutes longer, until fork-tender.

To serve: Serve the warm apples on individual plates, spooning the sauce from the pan over them and topping with vanilla ice cream.

# Tres Leches Cake with Mango and Lime

SERVES 12

PER SERVING: 280 CALORIES, 10 GRAMS FAT
PER SERVING (SUGAR FREE): 160 CALORIES, 5 GRAMS FAT

## cake

Nonstick pan spray

1¾ cups cake flour

1½ teaspoons baking powder

½ teaspoon salt

⅓ cup plus 1 tablespoon 2% milk,
    at room temperature

¼ cup canola oil

1 teaspoon pure vanilla extract

2 large eggs, at room temperature

½ cup sugar

3 egg whites from large eggs,
    at room temperature

SWEET
& SUGAR
FREE!

Substitute Sugar-Free Sponge
Cake (page 38) for the cake. For
the filling, increase the evaporated
milk to 1¼ cups and substitute
¼ cup plus 1 tablespoon agave
nectar for the sweetened condensed milk. For the topping,
substitute ¾ teaspoon (1 packet) of
Truvía for the sugar. To assemble,
pour half of the hot milk mixture
over one cake layer. Top with the
second layer, then pour the
remaining milk filling over the top.

A Day of the Dead celebration would not be the same without Tres Leches, the sponge cake soaked in three types of milk and crowned with whipped cream. The cake is popular year-round in Mexico and many South American countries. Thanks to the state's large Latino population, it is often found in taquerias and in Mexican bakeries and markets in California. The Day of the Dead follows Halloween. Topped with fans of bright orange mango and thin slices of lime, this cake is perfect for either occasion.

To make the cake: Preheat the oven to 350°F with a rack in the center position. Coat a 9-inch square cake pan with pan spray.

Sift the flour, baking powder, and salt into a small bowl. In another small bowl, whisk the milk, oil, and vanilla. Set the bowls aside.

Using an electric mixer, beat the eggs on high speed until they are foamy. Gradually add ¼ cup of the sugar, a few spoonfuls at a time. Beat for 4 minutes longer, until the mixture is thick and pale. Sift the flour mixture over the top and use a spatula to fold it in. Fold in the milk mixture just until it is incorporated.

Using a standing mixer fitted with the whisk attachment, beat the egg whites on high speed until they are foamy. (Alternatively, use a hand-held electric mixer.) Gradually add the remaining ¼ cup sugar, a few teaspoons at a time. Beat until medium peaks form, curling over softly when you lift the beater.

recipe continues

## tres leches filling

1 cup fat-free evaporated milk

½ cup plus 1 tablespoon nonfat
    sweetened condensed milk

¼ cup plus 2 tablespoons 2% milk

1½ teaspoons finely grated lime
    zest

## topping

½ cup plus 1 tablespoon heavy
    cream

½ cup plus 1 tablespoon nonfat
    sour cream

2 tablespoons sugar

2 teaspoons finely grated lime zest

1 teaspoon fresh lime juice

2 ripe small mangos, peeled,
    seeded, and cut into ¼-inch-
    thick slices, for garnish

1 lime, unpeeled, cut into ⅛-inch-
    thick rounds, for garnish

MAKE AHEAD!

The cake can be made a day
ahead and kept, covered, at room
temperature. After pouring the hot
filling over the cake, it can be
refrigerated overnight before
finishing.

Fold the egg whites into the batter just until there are no visible white streaks. Spread the batter evenly in the prepared pan. Bake for 25 minutes, until the top is golden and a toothpick inserted into the center comes out clean. Transfer the pan to a wire rack and let the cake cool completely in the pan.

To make the filling: In a small saucepan, whisk together the evaporated milk, condensed milk, and 2% milk. Whisk in the lime zest. Heat the mixture over medium heat until it is steaming. Poke the cooled cake all over with a fork, and then pour the hot filling evenly over it. Cover the cake and refrigerate for several hours, until most of the liquid has been absorbed.

To make the topping: Use an electric mixer to beat the heavy cream on high speed until very firm peaks form. On low speed, mix in the sour cream, sugar, lime zest, and lime juice.

To finish: Run a knife around the inside of the cake pan, pressing against the cake to loosen it. Invert the cake onto a serving platter. Spoon the whipped topping over the cake to cover the top but not the sides. Fan the mango and lime slices over the topping.

To serve: Present the cake whole. Then cut it into 4 pieces in one direction and 3 in the other to make 12 pieces.

Refrigerate any leftover cake, tightly covered, for up to 4 days.

# Pumpkin-Ricotta Cheesecake

SERVES 12

PER SERVING: 221 CALORIES, 9.5 GRAMS FAT

PER SERVING (SUGAR FREE): 158 CALORIES, 10 GRAMS FAT

Nonstick pan spray

Dough for 1 Shortbread Cookie Crust (page 28) or for 1 Quick Graham Cracker Crust (page 25)

8 ounces (1 cup) reduced-fat cream cheese (neufchâtel), preferably Kraft brand

1 cup sugar

⅓ cup nonfat sour cream, at room temperature

2 large eggs, at room temperature

2 egg whites from large eggs, at room temperature

1 teaspoon pure vanilla extract

⅔ cup canned pumpkin puree

½ teaspoon ground cinnamon

¼ teaspoon ground nutmeg

¼ teaspoon ground ginger

¼ teaspoon salt

⅛ teaspoon ground cloves

1 cup plus 2 tablespoons reduced-fat ricotta cheese

2 tablespoons large pecan pieces, toasted, for garnish

2 tablespoons pomegranate seeds, for garnish

You might not expect to see cheesecake in a book called *Sweet & Skinny*, but the blend of pumpkin, ricotta, and spices puts this flavorful version low on the guilt scale. The Shortbread Cookie Crust (page 28) is worth the effort, but if you are short on time, the Quick Graham Cracker Crust (page 25) works well, too.

Preheat the oven to 325°F with a rack in the lower third of the oven. Coat a 9-inch springform cake pan with pan spray. Press the crust dough firmly into the bottom of the pan, and set it aside.

Using an electric mixer, beat the cream cheese and sugar on medium speed for 2 to 3 minutes, until it is completely smooth and well blended. (If using a standing mixer, use the paddle attachment.) Add the sour cream, eggs, egg whites, and vanilla; mix for 2 to 3 minutes longer to blend well. Scrape down the sides of the bowl as needed. Add the pumpkin, cinnamon, nutmeg, ginger, salt, and cloves and mix for 1 minute longer. Add the ricotta and mix just until it is incorporated.

Pour the batter over the crust and bake for 50 to 60 minutes, until the cheesecake jiggles only slightly in the center when you gently shake the pan. (If the cheesecake browns too quickly or begins to crack, tent a piece of aluminum foil over the top, without touching the filling, for the remaining baking time.)

SWEET
& SUGAR
FREE!

Substitute 5 tablespoons plus 1 teaspoon (20 packets) of Truvía for the sugar in the filling, and use the sugar-free version of the shortbread crust.

Transfer the pan to a wire rack and let it cool for 1 hour. Then run a knife around the edge of the pan if needed to loosen the cheesecake, remove the outer pan ring, and transfer the cake, on its base, to a serving plate. Cover the cake loosely with plastic film and refrigerate for at least 3 hours or overnight.

*To serve:* Cut the cheesecake into 12 wedges, and garnish them with the toasted pecans and pomegranate seeds.

Refrigerate any leftover cheesecake, tightly covered, for up to 3 days.

# Red Currant-Raspberry Linzer Torte

SERVES 8

PER SERVING: 320 CALORIES, 13 GRAMS FAT

Nonstick pan spray

⅔ cup skin-on hazelnuts or almonds, toasted and cooled

1 cup plus 2 tablespoons all-purpose flour

⅓ cup plus 1 tablespoon sugar

1 teaspoon unsweetened Dutch-processed cocoa powder

½ teaspoon ground cinnamon

⅛ teaspoon ground cloves

⅛ teaspoon salt

¼ cup Browned Butter (page 24)

1 tablespoon non-hydrogenated vegetable shortening, such as Spectrum brand

¼ cup nonfat milk

⅔ cup red currant jelly

½ cup raspberry jam

During World War II, my *oma* (paternal grandmother) headed west out of Germany on foot, and she continued to walk for eight long months with my three-year-old father in tow. She left most everything behind, but carried with her the handwritten cookbook of her master-chef father as a keepsake. Linzer torte is typically made with raspberry jam only. I follow the family tradition, documented in my great-grandfather's book, of adding red currant jelly as well. It brightens the torte and enhances the flavors of the nuts and subtle spices.

Coat a 9 × 1-inch round tart pan with a removable bottom with pan spray.

Process the nuts in a food processor until they are very fine, stopping short of making nut paste. Add the flour, sugar, cocoa powder, cinnamon, cloves, and salt; pulse to combine well.

In a small saucepan, melt the browned butter and shortening over medium heat. (Alternatively, use a microwave oven.) With the food processor running, add the melted butter mixture to the flour mixture through the feed tube, mixing until it is incorporated. Add the milk through the feed tube and continue to mix until the dough clumps up around the blade.

Lay out a large piece of plastic film on a flat surface and turn the dough out onto the film. Knead the dough briefly to form a ball, then flatten it into a disk. Cover the disk with plastic film and roll it out to a 13-inch round that is a little over ⅛-inch thick.

recipe continues

**MAKE AHEAD!**

The lined tart pan and pastry disk can be frozen, tightly wrapped in plastic film, for up to 2 weeks in advance; let thaw overnight in the refrigerator before finishing.

Remove the top film and flip the dough over the prepared tart pan, centering it over the pan. Use the plastic film, now on top, as an aid to ease the dough into the bottom and sides of the pan. Peel off the film. Remove the overhanging dough by rolling the pin over the edges of the pan; reserve the scraps. If the pastry cracks or tears while lining the tart pan, use scraps of dough to patch it.

Roll the reserved dough scraps between sheets of plastic film into a 9-inch disk, about ⅛ inch thick. Freeze the lined tart pan and the disk for 20 minutes, until the dough is firm to the touch but not frozen through.

Preheat the oven to 375°F with a rack in the lower third of the oven.

In a small bowl, stir together the jelly and jam. Then spread the mixture evenly over the bottom of the chilled torte shell.

Use a pastry wheel, pizza cutter, or sharp knife to cut the reserved disk into eleven ½-inch-wide strips. Evenly space 6 strips over the filling, running horizontally. Press the edges of each strip firmly against the bottom crust to seal them. Lay 5 strips across the first set, running vertically, again spacing them evenly. Press to seal.

Bake for 30 to 35 minutes, until the crust is deep brown and the filling is bubbling. Let the torte cool on a wire rack for 20 minutes.

Run a paring knife along the inside of the pan to loosen any filling that may have seeped in between the pan and the torte. Center the torte pan over a glass or small bowl and let the pan sides drop away. Let the torte cool completely at room temperature, uncovered, at least 2 hours.

*To serve:* Cut the torte into 8 wedges.

Refrigerate any leftover torte, tightly covered, for up to 5 days.

# Crème Caramel

PER SERVING: 280 CALORIES, 6 GRAMS FAT

¾ cup sugar

¾ cup plus 2 tablespoons fat-free sweetened condensed milk

⅔ cup half-and-half

1⅓ cups 2% milk

2 large eggs

2 egg whites from large eggs

½ teaspoon pure vanilla extract

My mother has never had much of a sweet tooth, but a good crème caramel has always been her weakness. This recipe is her favorite Mother's Day dessert. For a twist, replace the vanilla with ¾ teaspoon instant espresso powder.

Preheat the oven to 325°F with a rack in the center position. Place six 4-ounce ramekins or custard cups in a 13 × 9-inch baking pan.

In a small nonreactive (stainless steel or copper) saucepan, stir together the sugar and ¼ cup water to completely moisten the sugar. Bring the mixture to a boil over medium heat, and use a pastry brush dipped in cold water to brush any sugar crystals from the sides of the pan. After the sugar dissolves and the mixture is clear and bubbling, raise the heat to medium-high. Cook until the sugar turns a light golden color. Divide the caramel among the ramekins, evenly covering the bottoms.

In a large bowl, whisk together the sweetened condensed milk, half-and-half, 2% milk, whole eggs, egg whites, and vanilla. Whisk vigorously for several minutes to thoroughly combine. Divide the custard evenly among the six ramekins.

Cover the baking pan with aluminum foil, sealing the foil tightly on three sides and leaving it lifted on the fourth side. Place the pan on the oven rack with the open edge closest to you, and pour warm water into the pan to reach halfway up the sides of the ramekins. Seal the open side.

**MAKE AHEAD!**

Mix the custard and refrigerate it, tightly covered, for up to 2 days in advance. Whisk well before pouring the custard into the ramekins.

Bake the custards for 40 to 45 minutes, until no longer jiggly. (Lift the foil carefully when checking, to avoid a burst of steam.)

Transfer the pan to a wire rack to cool and carefully remove the foil. When they are cool enough to handle, transfer the ramekins from the water bath to a baking sheet. Lightly cover them with plastic film and refrigerate for at least 3 hours or overnight.

Use your fingers to gently pull the custard from the sides of each ramekin to loosen it. Invert a small plate over one ramekin. Flip the ramekin and plate together, and give the ramekin a firm shake to release the custard onto the plate. Repeat with the remaining ramekins.

# sources & resources

Baking should be a joy, not a hassle, so I have created the recipes in this book using ingredients that are widely available in supermarkets and natural food stores, such as Whole Foods. Still, in some parts of the country, a particular ingredient or piece of equipment may be difficult to find. This resource list should help you find anything that is not available to you locally.

**FAGE YOGURT:** www.FageUsa.com

**GUITTARD CHOCOLATE:** www.Guittard.com

**KERRYGOLD BUTTER:** www.KerryGold.com

**KRAFT NEUFCHÂTEL CHEESE:** www.KraftBrands.com

**MEZZETTA OLIVE OIL:** www.Mezzetta.com

**MICROPLANE GRATERS:** us.Microplane.com

**OLAVE OLIVE OIL:** www.BelCantoFoods.com

**PLUGRÁ BUTTER:** www.Plugra.com

**SILPAT SILICONE BAKING MATS:** www.Silpat.com

**SMART BALANCE COOKING OIL:** www.SmartBalance.com

**SPECTRUM ORGANICS SHORTENING:** www.SpectrumOrganics.com

**SPICES AND EXTRACTS:** www.MySpiceSage.com

**TRUVÍA SWEETENER:** www.Truvia.com

**VANILLA EXTRACT AND BEANS:** www.TopVanilla.com; www.Vanilla.com

**WILLIAMS-SONOMA KITCHENWARE:** www.Williams-Sonoma.com

# acknowledgments

I thank my wonderful agent, Carole Bidnick, who always goes above and beyond her role. Thank you to Emily Takoudes at Clarkson Potter—your enthusiasm for the project has been amazing. My appreciation extends to the entire Clarkson Potter team, including Peggy Paul and designer Jenny Davis.

My heartfelt thanks go to Jennie Schacht, who worked diligently through multiple editorial cycles, and under tight deadlines, to help write and rewrite the manuscript, assuring a place for every word and every word in its place. You have been amazing to work with!

Special thanks to Cheryl Lew of Montclair Baking, who painstakingly tested the recipes. And thanks to Cathy Huang and Elizabeth Chaffin, who tested recipes and provided invaluable insight as home bakers. Thanks to Holly Stewart for putting so much time and care into the photography, and to food stylist Sandra Cook and hairstylist Dawn Sutti—together you made the food and me look beautiful.

To the Table 12 gang—Laura Werlin, Susie Biehler, and Michele Mandell—thank you for all your help and support. Thank you to my friend and manager, John Fuller, who has had my back since day one. Who else would personally deliver fifty pounds of cereal to me for an episode of *Food Network Challenge*?

So many friends have lent their support on this book and throughout the years, too many to mention them all by name, but I am so grateful and I thank you all!

Finally, I thank my mother for insisting we read *The Little Engine That Could,* instilling in me the mantra "I think I can, I think I can." I thank my father, who has been my willing guinea pig ever since I was barely tall enough to reach the stove, my *yiayia,* who was the first person to teach me how to cook, and my *oma,* who taught me to have nerves of steel in the kitchen—I love you all.

# index

NOTE: Page references in *italics* refer to photographs.